M000308985

THE
VISION
OF THE
BUILDING
OF THE
CHURCH

WITNESS LEE

Living Stream Ministry
Anaheim, CA • www.lsm.org

First Edition, March 2003.

ISBN 0-7363-2248-5

Published by

Living Stream Ministry
2431 W. La Palma Ave., Anaheim, CA 92801 U.S.A.
P. O. Box 2121, Anaheim, CA 92814 U.S.A.

Printed in the United States of America

03 04 05 06 07 08 09 / 9 8 7 6 5 4 3 2 1

CONTENTS

PREFACE

In a conference held in the church in Taipei in January 1961, Brother Witness Lee released ten messages focusing on the vision revealed in the holy Scriptures concerning the building of the church. The messages were full of light and power and were blessed by the Lord in an unprecedented way. Nearly the whole congregation offered themselves to God to be built up in the church. This book contains notes that were taken during those messages and that were slightly polished. Although the book has not been reviewed by the speaker, it is being published at this time to meet the present need. May the Lord grant us His blessing by revealing these timely messages to the spirit of every reader.

The Editorial Section
Taiwan Gospel Book Room
June 1964

CHAPTER ONE

THE VISION IN THE FIRST TWO CHAPTERS OF THE SCRIPTURES

Scripture Reading: Gen. 1:26-28; 2:7-12, 16, 18-24; Rev. 21:2-3, 9-14, 18-19, 21-24; 22:1-5; 4:2-3

We worship God that we could have this conference to concentrate our attention on this one topic—the building of the church. If we carefully read the Word from the beginning to the end in the light of God, we will see that the building of the church is a great revelation shown throughout the Scriptures. To reveal this matter requires the entire Bible. Therefore, we will cover many verses from the Scriptures, all of which are very important and which you must read carefully and attentively. Furthermore, as you review, ruminate over, and reflect on these messages before the Lord, I hope that you would check and refer to the verses. In this way, your understanding of these messages will be clearer and more thorough.

There is one matter concerning these meetings that requires a special explanation. For the release of the vision of the building, we will not have the meetings as we did in the past—always caring for the apprehension of the audience. Instead, we will simply do our best to release this glorious vision from the Word of God from an objective standpoint. Our prayer is that this vision will be released clearly and thoroughly. Therefore, we will not be able to take care of any other need. Concerning this, we ask that you would do your best to cooperate with us and to render us your help. I have a deep sense before the Lord that a very heavy burden is upon me to reveal to the children of God the vision of the mystery concerning the eternal purpose of God. This is not an easy task. Human words are not sufficient to convey this matter, and human thoughts are inadequate for understanding it. Therefore, I hope that while you are listening, you would also be looking to the Lord that He would support the one serving as His mouthpiece so that the one speaking may be able to thoroughly release the vision according to the Lord's plan and arrangement.

NEEDING A TRANSCENDENT VIEW
OF THE GLORIOUS VISION

In this conference I have a deep expectation that you would be carried away to a high place, far above all, to have a far-reaching view of God's vision. In Revelation when the apostle John saw the vision of Babylon, the corrupted city, he was in the wilderness, a place of desolation. However, in order to see the New Jerusalem, the glorious, holy city, he was brought by an angel to a high mountain. This was because the view from the plain was not adequate. He needed to be brought to a mountain, a high place, a transcendent realm, that he might have a sufficiently far-reaching and great view. Therefore, I earnestly look to the Lord in His presence that He would bring us all up to a high mountain, a high place, and release every one of us from ourselves, bringing us out of our own experiences, learning, and past attainments and lifting us up to a new realm, an elevated sphere, that we have never reached before so that we would have a transcendent view of the glorious vision of God.

We must realize that the visions in the book of Revelation were revealed by God to a deeply and highly experienced person—the apostle John. When John saw the visions on the island of Patmos, all the other apostles had already died, and he was the only one left. He was the last of the original twelve apostles remaining. He truly was a highly qualified person, yet God wanted to show him a new vision never before seen by man, a great and far-reaching vision, a high and transcendent vision. Therefore, God had to put him on an island in isolation. Furthermore, God had to carry him away from the plain and even away from himself onto the top of a high mountain for him to see the vision. How I wish that every brother and sister would have such an attitude and desire and that we would tell the Lord, "I want to be released and carried away from myself. I want to be freed not only from my wicked sins but also from my good, spiritual experiences. Although I have had many attainments already, I want to see a vision that is higher, greater, deeper, richer, and more far-reaching and transcendent." May God have mercy on every one of us that we would be rescued and carried away from ourselves to a transcendent position that we may have a transcendent view, a far-reaching sight, to see through all things so that we may see the glorious vision of God.

THE THREE SECTIONS OF THE HOLY SCRIPTURES

We have said that the entire Bible is required to prove and reveal this vision. If we carefully read through the Scriptures from beginning to end and consider them in a good way before God, calming our spirit to look to God, then we will clearly see that the first two chapters of the Bible (Gen. 1—2) form one section and that the last two chapters (Rev. 21—22) also form one section. These two sections, the beginning and the end of the entire Bible, mirror each other from afar. In between these two sections is another section from Genesis 3 through Revelation 20, which is the main body of the Bible. This section is like an interlude in a play, within which are many plots and events, twists and turns, ups and downs, and touching stories. To summarize it briefly, this section simply deals with matters on the positive side and matters on the negative side. These two sides, the positive and the negative, each emphasize three matters. By pointing out these three matters, we will see a sketch or outline of this section.

The Major Section in the Middle Having Two Aspects—the Positive and the Negative— with Six Crucial Points

Genesis 3 is the start or beginning of this inserted section. This section starts by telling us that a serpent came in. The first two chapters of Genesis speak of how God created the heavens, the earth, and all things, including the highest of the created, living things—the human race—as the center of the universe. They also tell how God created man with His image to be His representative and how He put this man before the tree of life so that he would become a man of honor and glory. This is the description in the first two chapters. Following this, chapter three opens with a description of a serpent. We all know that this serpent was Satan in disguise. When this serpent came, he injected his poison into the man whom God had created in His own image and for His own glory. The poison that the serpent injected into man is the sin that is within man. The sin that dwells in us and is referred to in Romans 7 is the poison of the serpent in Genesis 3. This poison acts, reigns, and subdues us. From this sin many sinful acts are produced. Since man has this sin-causing poison within him, he is held captive and controlled by it. Hence, man cannot help but commit many sinful acts. Because of these sins, death follows. Therefore, death comes to all men. The serpent came, he injected sin into man, and from sin came death. These are the three most important items on the negative side in Genesis 3 through Revelation 20.

In this long section of the Bible we often see the "head" or the "tail" of the serpent appear. In many portions we see the serpent coming out of man. Sometimes we see his tail, and other times we see his head. When John the Baptist and the Lord Jesus were on the earth, they called those who followed Satan "offspring of vipers" (Matt. 3:7; 12:34). In the Old Testament, the children of Israel, one time while journeying through the wilderness, did something that offended God. Then poisonous serpents came and bit them, so they called on God to rescue them. God told Moses to make a brass serpent and hang it on a pole. These are two stories related to the serpent. Then the serpent is mentioned again in Revelation 12, where he is called "the ancient serpent" (v. 9). He is called this because he was already in existence at the time of the garden of Eden. Then in Revelation 20 we see the Lord Jesus in His victorious power binding the poisonous serpent and casting him into the bottomless pit and, subsequently, into the lake of fire. Therefore, this section of the Bible begins with the serpent coming into the garden of Eden and ends with the serpent being cast into the lake of fire.

If you were to ask me what this long section of the Bible from Genesis 3 to Revelation 20 is about, I would tell you that on the negative side it is about all of the issues of the serpent's coming into the midst of man and into man himself. I once saw in a Christian book a chart of the seven dispensations. It showed the periods of time from Cain to the end of the millennial kingdom. Above all of these periods of time, there was a huge serpent. It stretched from the first dispensation all the way to the end of the millennium. That chart expressed this point perfectly. The story of man on the earth throughout the ages, beginning with the sin of Adam and ending with the millennial kingdom, is truly the story of all the troubles caused by the serpent. Throughout history the serpent comes and goes; he manifests himself and then retreats. Sometimes he shows his head, other times he shows his tail, and still other times he shows a part of his body. On the earth the serpent continually causes men to sin, causing them to be brought into death. If you read the newspaper, you will see that not one day goes by without an occurrence of robbery, adultery, fornication, theft, or murder. Whenever I read these reports, I always have the feeling that these reports are stories of men who have been poisoned by the serpent and that all these events happened because of the serpent's poison. This society has been occupied by the serpent. Therefore, it is natural that it is full of sins, corruption, and death. This is the Bible's description of the negative situation. The serpent entered in Genesis 3, and it is not until Revelation 20 that he will be cast into the eternal lake of fire. At that time the Lord will also judge all the sinners and all of the sins of men. Lastly, He will cast death into the lake of fire. These are the main items on the negative side that are spoken of in the Bible.

However, thanks be to God that on the earth we have not only night but also day and not only the negative side but also the positive side. We must worship Him that after the serpent entered in Genesis 3, God declared in the very same chapter that the seed of the woman would come and bruise the serpent's head. This One who would deal with the serpent would not be an ordinary man. Every ordinary man is a seed of man, but this One would be the seed of a woman. Today we all know that this seed of the woman is the Son of the living God, our glorious Lord Jesus, who was born through a virgin and who was also the most outstanding One among mankind. This One came and bruised the serpent's head. The Bible says that "the Son of God was manifested, that He might destroy the works of the devil" (1 John 3:8). The serpent came in, but afterward Christ also came in to deal with and get rid of the serpent. Since that time, a war has been going on among mankind on the earth—the war between the serpent and the Son of God. If you know this line in the Bible, then it will not be difficult to see from the Scriptures that the serpent was continually using all his devices to try to prevent the birth of this seed of the woman. On the other hand, you will also see that God was exercising all the authority of His sovereignty to put a restraint on the serpent's activity and that ultimately He made it possible for His Son to come to the earth through incarnation to deal with the serpent.

The serpent brought in sin, but Christ brought in righteousness. In fact, He Himself is righteousness. When we receive Him, we gain Him as our righteousness, and we are justified before God and delivered from sin. The serpent brought in death through sin, but this One, Christ, brought in life through righteousness. The serpent injected sin into man and thus trapped man in death, but Christ came and gave man righteousness and thus caused man to have life in righteousness. Christ is versus the serpent, righteousness is versus sin, and life is versus death. Although there are many plots and events, twists and turns, ups and downs, and bends and curves in this section of the Bible, it is a story played out by two main characters, and each of these main characters has two smaller, subordinate characters. In this story there is the serpent and the Son of God. These two continually oppose each other. With the serpent are sin and death, and with the Son of God are righteousness and life. I want this picture to be impressed into us. When we read the Bible, we should immediately be able to see what is the serpent, what is sin, and what is death, and we should also see what is Christ, what is righteousness, and what is life. These are the two sides that we must see when we read from Genesis 3 to Revelation 20. All the stories in this middle section are played out by these six characters.

THE FIRST AND LAST SECTIONS
CORRESPONDING TO ONE ANOTHER

Now we want to see how the first and last sections of the Bible correspond to one another. If we would calmly consider the beginning chapters of Genesis and the concluding chapters of Revelation, we would see that these two portions of the Word have four points that correspond with each other.

First, in the beginning, in Genesis 2, the Bible mentions the tree of life. Then in chapter three it says that this tree of life was locked up. From then on, there is no direct mention of the tree of life until the end of Revelation, where the tree of life appears again. Therefore, the tree of life is mentioned in the first section and the last section of the Bible. In one section it is referred to in the way of a beginning, and in the other section it is referred to in the way of a conclusion. Thus, these two sections correspond to one another.

Second, in both the first section and the last section of the Bible there is a river. Genesis 2 tells us that "a river went forth from Eden to water the garden" (v. 10). At the end of the Bible, Revelation says that a river of water of life proceeds out of the throne of God (22:1). These two rivers correspond with one another.

Third, in Genesis 2 three kinds of precious materials are mentioned—gold, bdellium, and onyx stone (vv. 11-12). At the end of Revelation, a city that is pure gold appears (21:18). Its street is pure gold, its gates are pearls, and its wall is adorned with precious stones (vv. 19-21). Thus, these three kinds of precious materials are also at the end. The only difference is that they have become a building. Thus, this is another aspect of how the two sections of the Bible, the beginning and the end, correspond with one another.

Fourth, the last item mentioned in Genesis 2 is a counterpart (vv. 18-24), and the central figure mentioned in the last two chapters of Revelation is also a counterpart—the bride, the wife of the Lamb (21:2, 9).

Therefore, the beginning and the end of the Bible clearly mention the same topics with the same items as their content and center. The tree of life, the river, the three kinds of precious materials, and the counterpart in one section correspond with the same items in the other section. All the items in the first section correspond with the items in the last section. No one can deny that this is the writing of the Holy Spirit.

All these corresponding items show us what God intends to have, what He wants to do in the universe, and what His focus and goal are. At the beginning of the Bible, there is a picture that clearly describes the desire of God, and at the end there is a picture that describes to us His desire as it will be when it is achieved and when He has gained what He wants. This picture is a city built with gold, pearl, and precious stones as the habitation of God and the counterpart of the Lamb. The long middle section of the Bible from Genesis 3 to Revelation 20 is the process, the interlude, within which are numerous twists and turns, plots and events, and moving stories.

THE VISION IN THE FIRST TWO CHAPTERS OF THE SCRIPTURES

The Background of the Creation of the Heavens, the Earth, and All Things

Now we want to see what the vision revealed in these two sections is and what the important points of the vision are, point by point. However, before I point these things out, let me first speak a little about the background.

Everyone who has read the Bible knows that the first two chapters of Genesis are a record of God's creation. God's creation is not a small matter. Rather, it is a great matter. Thus, the way God wrote about it is very marvelous. The Bible uses only two chapters to describe in a general way how God created the heavens, the earth, and all the things in the universe. Strictly speaking, these matters are covered only in one chapter—Genesis 1. Why is it that the record concerning God's creation in the Bible is so brief? This is because the divine record was written according to the central goal of God's intention. The goal of His intention is life. Therefore,

His record was written according to the view of life and with life as the goal.

Genesis 1:1 tells us that in the beginning God created the heavens and the earth. Verse 2 then says that the earth became waste and emptiness and that darkness was on the surface of the deep. This is a description of the background, showing us that at that time the earth was full of death, full of chaos, and void of life. It goes on to say that the Spirit of God came to brood upon the surface of the waters (v. 2b) and that following this the light came (v. 3). From our experience we know that the brooding of the Spirit of God is for life and that the illuminating of light is also for life. After the light came, there was the separation of the light from the darkness (v. 4), the separation of the waters under the expanse from the waters above the expanse (vv. 6-8), and the separation of the land from the waters (vv. 9-10). Originally, the universe had been in a state of confusion, but now there were separations. Once these separations had been made, the dry land emerged to generate life. The first kind of life that was generated was the lowest form of life—the plant life, which is without consciousness or feeling. Then the lower forms of animal life—the fish and the birds—were generated. Following this, the higher forms of animal life, consisting of the mammals, were generated. Finally, the highest creature, man, was generated. Among the created beings, man is the highest creature, having the image of God and the authority of God. However, man did not have the highest life, which is the uncreated life of God. Therefore, God put this highest creature before the tree of life, which was a type of Himself as the God of life, so that man could receive Him to become precious material. I believe that you all are clear that this is the background of the first two chapters of Genesis.

Now let us look at the important points concerning us human beings in the first two chapters of Genesis.

Man Collectively Being the Image and Representative of God

First, God created man according to His image and gave man the authority to rule over the creatures that were in the air, on the earth, and in the water. God gave man dominion over the sea, the land, and the air. We want to see a little concerning this matter of image and dominion. If you carefully read the Bible, you would see that Christ is the image of God. Therefore, the fact that man was created in the image of God means that man was created according to Christ. Man is the image of Christ. What is an image? An image is an expression. For God to have an image means that He has an expression. Christ being the image of God means that Christ is the expression of God. Man being the image of Christ means that man is the expression, the manifestation, of Christ. God is in His Son that His Son might be His image as His expression. God also created us according to His Son that we may be the image of His Son as the expression of His Son. After we are saved, the one thing God wants to do in every one of us is to cause each one of us to be conformed to the image of His Son. This work is not only a work of conformation but also a work of transformation. From the moment we are saved, the Holy Spirit within us, in coordination with the outward environment, transforms us daily so that we become more and more like Christ. Ultimately, when the Lord returns, we will be changed from the inside to the outside, from our spirit to our body, to be exactly like our glorious Lord. Then we will be wholly the same as Him. What is this for? This is for us to express Christ. To express Christ is to express God. God in Christ comes into us as the mold to conform us to His very form so that we may be His living image to express Him.

On the other hand, by reading the Bible we can also see that God's dominion is placed completely upon Christ. God gave Christ dominion over the whole universe so that Christ would have all the authority in the heavens and on earth and would act as God's representative, vested with full authority. We thank God that because we have believed in Christ, received Christ, and been joined to Christ, His authority has become our authority. On the day when Christ comes back to the earth to be King, the overcoming saints will be co-kings with Him to reign together with Him. Before that day arrives, the overcoming saints and the overcoming church must reign and rule over all things on the earth today with Christ in their spirit.

Therefore, the image of God is upon Christ, and God's authority is also upon Christ. The One who can express God is Christ, and the One who can represent God is also Christ. However, not only is Christ such a One, but today all of us who are in Christ are also such persons. Every one of us has the image of Christ and the authority of Christ. It is in Christ that we express God and represent God. God gave us His image in Christ, and God also gave us His authority in Christ. It is in Christ that a proper believer or a proper church has the image of God and the authority of God. Under normal conditions, people should be able to see God's image and expression in us, and they should also be able to see God's authority and representation.

Perhaps you would ask what this has to do with building. What I want to say is that in the beginning God created only one man in His image and wanted only one man as His representative. He did not create many men in His image, nor did He want many representatives. God did not create many Adams; rather, He created only one Adam. We must realize that the Adam whom God created was not merely a single Adam but a collective Adam. When Adam was created, were you and I in him? We all must acknowledge that when Adam was created, we were all in him. The Adam who was created was not a small Adam but a great Adam, a collective Adam, a corporate Adam. God did not want many individual Adams to be His image and to represent Him individually. Rather, God wanted the many Adams to become a great Adam collectively to be His one complete image and His one corporate representative. This implies the principle of building.

In this universe God wants only one collective image and one collective representative. God's intention is not that you would be an image, I would be an image, and another would also be an image. No, God's desire in Genesis 2 was that the descendants of Adam who were in Adam would all be the one unique image of God. Through this we can see the matter of building.

We all know that every saved person is an image of God.

This is right. However, we may have the concept that, as saved ones, we are individual images. I am an image individually, and another brother is also an image individually. Therefore, if there are 20,000 saved ones, then there are 20,000 images of God. This kind of concept is wrong. We must remember that regardless of how many thousands of saved ones there are, there is only one collective image and one collective representative. Both the image and the representation are in one great person. This is building, and this is coordination. We are not the many individual images of God. Rather, in our assembling together we are built together and coordinated together to become a great person as God's one complete image. If in the beginning God had created twenty-eight Adams or a hundred Adams, then today we could suggest that it would be all right for us to say that we are individually God's images. However, in the beginning God collected millions and millions of Adam's descendants and put them all in Adam to make them a great Adam as God's image. This image of God and representative of God is not the many scattered individuals. Rather, it is the one complete, great person, a collection of many, many persons to be God's unique image and unique representative in the universe. This is the building, the coordination, and the oneness.

Man Being an Earthen Vessel with a Spirit

Second, God formed man with the clay of the ground. Clay is of little value, but God used clay to form a man to be His vessel. I do not know whether or not you have ever thought about the fact that we humans are actually vessels and that we daily fill ourselves with many things. Whenever we eat and drink, we put things into us. Even this morning, as we are listening to the message, we are putting things into ourselves. We fill our mouths with food and water, our ears with sound, our eyes with scenery, and our noses with odors. Every day we fill ourselves with all kinds of things. We truly are vessels.

However, we must remember that we humans are able to take in more than food, water, sound, scenery, and odors. Within us is another part that can take in the mystical, spiritual God. When God created us, He created us not only with a stomach, ears, eyes, and a nose but also with a spirit. When He created us, He breathed the breath of life into us. When this breath of life came into us, it became something mysterious; it became the spirit within us. This spirit is a receiving organ, enabling us to receive the pneumatic God. Man is a vessel made of clay, but within man, this vessel of clay, there is a mechanism. Man may be likened to a radio. A radio may appear to be merely a wooden box, but it is different from other boxes because within it there is a mechanism that receives sound by receiving the invisible electromagnetic waves in the air. In the same manner, within this earthen vessel of ours is a very precious mechanism. As long as we set this mechanism properly and correctly, God, like the electrical waves, will come in. Oh, within man there is a spirit! This is a very special point in the record in Genesis. Why is there a spirit in man, who is made of clay? It is to enable man to receive God who is Spirit so that God as the Spirit can be put into man.

Receiving the Tree of Life as Food

Third, God put man, who was made of clay on the outside and who had a spirit inside, in front of the tree of life. If we read the Bible to the end, we will realize that this tree of life is God Himself, because God Himself is life. The Bible says that when the Lord Jesus came to the earth, "in Him was life" (John 1:4). The Bible also tells us that He is the bread of life to be taken in and eaten by man as life (6:48, 51). This is what we have been saying all along—God wants men to receive Him as food into them to be their life. It is not difficult to understand that the food we eat every day enters into us and becomes our nourishment and our constituents. Likewise, God comes into us to be our life so that He would become our constituents and would mingle Himself and unite Himself with us to become one with us.

THE RIVER FLOWING AND WATERING

Fourth, in the garden of Eden there was a river flowing and watering. This is a symbolic picture, and we must understand the meaning hidden in it. Before this the Bible says that there was a tree of life in the middle of the garden and that man was put in front of the tree in order that he would eat its fruit. Following this it says that there was a river flowing and watering therein. What is the meaning of this? This indicates that if you receive this life into you, this life will not only nourish you as food, enabling you to live, but it will also flow in you and water you as living water.

In today's universe, all the material things are symbols of spiritual things. If we merely eat dry food without drinking any water, then the food will not turn or move easily in the stomach and will surely cause us to feel uncomfortable. Thus, whenever we eat, we should not only take in dry food but also drink water, milk, soup, or other liquids. In this way the stomach will receive the nourishment, and the food can flow and be digested. We must remember that Genesis chapter two is a picture. In this picture there is not only the tree of life as food but also a river flowing and watering. Therefore, in the Gospel of John the Lord Jesus not only said that He was the bread from heaven for people to eat and not be hungry; He also said that if anyone was thirsty, he should come to Him to drink and that he who drank the water that He gave would never thirst again, but this water would become a fountain of living water in him gushing up into eternal life (4:14). He is not only the bread of life but also the water of life. The bread of life is for our nourishment, and the water of life is for us to be watered.

PRODUCING GOLD, BDELLIUM, AND PRECIOUS STONE

Fifth, wherever the river flows and waters, it produces pure gold, bdellium, and precious stone. This is also a picture. Because we all have a certain amount of spiritual experience, it should not be difficult for us to understand what is implied in this picture. When we receive the Lord as the bread of life and as the living water, His life enters into us to flow and to water us, with the result that we have pure gold within. Most readers of the Bible agree that in typology pure gold denotes the nature of God. God's life, God's nature, and God's substance are the pure gold in the universe. When the Lord comes into us, He comes into us as our life to satisfy our hunger, to quench our thirst, and to flow in us, but at the same time He also brings the nature and substance of God into us. Thus, we gain the treasure of the universe.

Therefore, we truly must praise the Lord. Although we are made of clay and are earthen vessels, today we have pure gold within us. We should all jump up and shout, "We have pure gold within us! We have pure gold within us!" Pure gold is our inner substance and our inner nature. We should never consider ourselves too lowly.

Sometimes we may meet a very uncultured brother who may not have much education, may speak in an unclear way, and may do things awkwardly. However, when we fellowship with him and pray with him, we discover that there is gold within him and that, as Paul said, there is a treasure in the earthen vessel. Who is this treasure? This treasure is the God who is gold. We have nothing to boast about in ourselves as earthen vessels, but we should always praise God for the gold within.

This is where our worth is. A Christian's worth is that he has Christ within him, that he has God within him. This God who is in Christ is our treasure. He is our pure gold. Outwardly, we Christians are no different from the people on the street. They are earthen vessels, and we also are earthen vessels. However, inwardly, there is a great difference between them and us. We have gold within us, but they do not. They are altogether earthen, without and within. We, however, are earthen on the outside, but we are not earthen on the inside. Outwardly we are earthen vessels, but within there is gold.

I will never forget the day in 1939 when I was in Tientsin and saw this vision. I hit the table and shouted, "Hallelujah, God is in me!" Then I ran downstairs and went out to the street. I almost wanted to shout to the people on the street, saying, "Do not touch me! If you touch me, you touch God! I am truly great! I have God in me!" That day I was like a crazy person because I had seen the vision that I had God within me and that this God was the pure gold within me.

The flowing of God's life in man issues not only in gold but also in bdellium. In the Old Testament, bdellium is mentioned only twice. The first mention is in the second chapter of Genesis, and the other mention is in Numbers 11:7. Some Jewish rabbis and authorities of the Hebrew language suggest that the word for *bdellium* in Hebrew denotes a kind of coagulation of the sap that flows out of a resinous tree, its brightness and solidity resembling that of a pearl. Others say that this word denotes a pearl. Whether the word *bdellium* denotes resin or pearl, the principle is the same. A pearl is produced when an oyster in the sea is wounded by a grain of sand. The oyster then secretes a kind of life juice to cover the grain of sand, and after a long time, this grain of sand becomes a pearl. Resin is produced when a tree is wounded and exudes something from within that solidifies. Therefore, these two materials both typify the Lord. This wounded One can be said to be of the plant kingdom or of the animal kingdom, because some places in the Scriptures use plants to typify the Lord, while other places use animals to typify the Lord. Our Lord was wounded, His body was pierced, and the life fluid flowed out from Him and flowed to us. Now, we humans as grains of sand are being transformed into bright pearls of worth. Once we receive the Lord into us as our life, we are regenerated and have the transforming life. Once we receive God as our gold, His life and our life mingle together, causing us to be transformed into pearl. This is the beginning. Therefore, in the New Jerusalem the pearl is an entrance, a gate, as a beginning.

After the pearl, there is the precious stone. The onyx stone in Genesis 2 is a kind of mineral, like diamonds, precious gems, and jade. These stones were not originally created as precious stones. Rather, they were things that were originally created but that passed through high pressure and intense heat and were transformed into precious materials. Therefore, this indicates that from the moment we receive God's life, gain the gold, and receive the transformation of the pearl through regeneration, the Holy Spirit starts to do the work of pressing and burning upon us, within us, and in our circumstances, thereby transforming us so that we show forth the glory of God.

Due to the moving of the Holy Spirit in us and His discipline through the environment, that is, the coordination of the inward and outward working to press us and burn us, there is hardly any true, God-loving child of God who does not have problems. A Christian often has many difficulties. Sometimes they are like an intense fire burning him, and sometimes they are like heavy weights pressing down on him. Although he may pray much about them, it often seems as if God does not hear him. The reason can only be that God wants to put this earthen vessel in the furnace to purify it. Without passing through this process of burning and pressing, this one who is like wood, clay, and sand could not be transformed into precious stone. The precious stone is produced little by little, and it increases little by little. In the New Jerusalem the wall is built with precious stones. When the wall is built up, then the city is completed. Similarly, when every one of us, in God's hand and in the Holy Spirit, has been transformed under high pressure and intense heat into precious stones, then we must believe that the building of God is about to be completed. Formerly we were earthen Adams, vessels of clay. However, when we receive God in Christ into us as our life and as we allow this life to flow in us and allow the Holy Spirit to do the burning, pressing, and transforming work on us, we as earthen vessels will not only have gold, but we will also be transformed into pearls and precious stones. In this way we will become precious materials.

Being Built as the Counterpart of Christ

Besides the matter of transformation, there is also the matter of building in Genesis 2. After these precious materials have been produced, the goal is not to leave them scattered. Rather, they are to be built together and coordinated into a corporate entity as a counterpart. Therefore, Genesis 2, after speaking about gold, pearl, and precious stone, speaks about a counterpart. If you read only Genesis 2, it is hard to see that this counterpart comes from the collective building together of the pure gold, pearl, and precious stones. However, when you read the concluding portion of Revelation, you will see that the holy city, which is the wife of the Lamb and the bride of the Lamb, is built with pure gold, pearls, and precious stones.

Brothers and sisters, now we must conclude this message.

I hope that every child of God would see what God wants to do in us. We must see that God wants us to collectively be His image and representative. Although we are persons made of clay, we have a spirit within us. We should receive Him into us, eat Him, drink Him, and enjoy Him daily as our bread of life, allowing this life to flow and water us as living water. In this way, we will be transformed in God's life and in Christ. Day by day the earthen nature will be discharged, and we will be changed from glory to glory into the same glorious image of the Lord, eventually arriving at a condition in which we are completely transformed into pure gold, pearl, and precious stone. It seems very good to arrive at this stage, but it is still not sufficient. There is still the final matter of being built up. Even after we have arrived at such a stage of spiritual maturity, we still need one thing—to be built together with all the saints that we may become the counterpart of God and the bride of Christ.

I truly hope that God's children would all see this vision. I say again that God wants a corporate image for His expression and a corporate authority to represent Him. As those who were created in Adam, we are like earthen vessels, and we are also scattered. If we would like to become God's image to express Him and be God's authority to represent Him, we must continually receive Him into us with our spirit and our heart. Then we also have to learn to enjoy Him by eating and drinking Him every day. We also should allow Him to flow in us so that more and more we would have the element of gold in us and be transformed into pearl. Furthermore, we must submit to the burning and pressing in the hand of the Holy Spirit and in the environment arranged by the Holy Spirit so that our worthless being may undergo a glorious transformation to become precious stone. What a glorious matter! Finally, we must see that we, being precious materials, are not to be left scattered around. Instead, we should be corporately built together into a living, built-up entity. Such an entity will be a city, a house, and a Body built by God, and it will also be His glorious, loving counterpart. It is only in this way that God can be expressed and represented and His heart's desire can be satisfied.

CHAPTER TWO

THE SCENE OF THE NEW JERUSALEM

Scripture Reading: Rev. 21:2-3, 9-14, 18-19, 21-24; 22:1-5; 4:3

We have clearly said that the first two chapters of the Bible describe a picture and that the last two chapters also describe a picture. These two pictures placed at the beginning and at the end of the Bible correspond with each other from afar. In this message I would like to review this point with you once more.

THE GLORIOUS GOAL OF GOD

We have seen that the first two chapters of Genesis show us how God created the heavens and the earth as the realm, all the creatures in it as the means, and man as the center among all the creatures. God created man so that man would be His image to express Him and have His authority to represent Him. Image and dominion are God's two goals regarding man in the universe. However, although God's intention is for man to express Him and represent Him, He does not want man to do it individually in a scattered and independent manner. Rather, He wants all those who have been saved by grace to gather together so that they would all become one man. He wants many people to become a corporate, great, and universal man to be God's one corporate image, God's one universal expression, and God's one universal representative.

We have also seen that God's image is Christ (Col. 1:15) and that God's authority is vested in Christ (Matt. 28:18). God's image and God's authority converge in our glorious Lord Christ. No one has ever seen God. However, this Christ, the only begotten Son of God, who is in the bosom of the Father, has declared Him (John 1:18). He is the effulgence of

God's glory and the impress of God's substance (Heb. 1:3a). As such, He expresses all that God is in a complete way. He is also truly God's representative in the universe, all of God's authority having been vested in Him, laid upon His shoulders, and placed in His hand. Thank and praise God that now Christ has been enlarged. Through death and resurrection Christ enlarged and spread Himself into us who have believed and received Him. Today every one of us has Christ within. Today this Christ is an enlarged Christ. Everyone who has received Christ as life bears the image of Christ, which is the image of God. At the same time, everyone also has the authority of Christ, which is the authority of God. Furthermore, we who have Christ neither bear Christ's image nor exercise Christ's authority in a scattered, independent, or individual way. Rather, we all have become members that have been aggregated together into one Body bearing Christ's image and exercising Christ's authority.

This Body is the mystical Body of Christ, and the Head is Christ Himself. This mystical Body with the mystical Head becomes a mystical, universal great man as described in Ephesians 5:32, which says, "This mystery is great, but I speak with regard to Christ and the church." God Himself dwells in this mystical man, and all the fullness of the Godhead dwells bodily in this mystical man. This mystical man is a vessel for God's expression, a living image of God expressing God in the universe. At the same time, this mystical man, having been joined to Christ and having Christ as the Head, has the authority that God committed to Christ and can therefore represent God on the earth to deal with the power of darkness and subdue all the forces that rebel against God. Therefore, the church is the Body of Christ, joined to Christ as one, with a glorious commission to be God's image to express God on the one hand and to have God's authority to represent God on the other. This is the glorious goal of God shown in the first two chapters of Genesis.

FOUR STEPS TO ATTAIN GOD'S GOAL

After seeing God's goal, we may wonder how the man created by God can attain this goal. How can the man created

by God become a living image of God and practically have the
authority of God? This is a question concerning the way to
attain this goal. Genesis 2, following chapter one, speaks concerning the way. The presentation of the way may seem to be
very simple, but it is actually very detailed and clear.

The First Step—
Creating Man and Putting a Spirit in Him

The first step that Genesis 2 shows us is the step of God
forming man out of dust. Man was an earthen vessel, a vessel
made of dust. However, within this man who was made of
dust, God created a spirit. This is the most distinctive feature
of man, distinguishing man from all the other creatures. The
reason man surpasses all the other creatures and is the highest among the creatures is because man has this excellent
spirit within him. Although man is an earthen body outwardly,
within him is an excellent spirit. The reason God created
this excellent spirit for man was so that man would have a
spirit to contact and receive God who is Spirit. As we have
illustrated, a radio is a mere wooden box outwardly, but
inwardly it contains a component that is capable of receiving
electromagnetic waves. Since the component is able to receive
the electromagnetic waves from the air, the electromagnetic
waves will cause a response in this component as long as it is
tuned to the right frequency. In the same manner, as human
beings of visible substance, we are like earthen boxes, but
within us there is a precious and excellent spirit. This spirit
is the spiritual component within us that enables us to
receive God who is Spirit.

The Second Step—
Putting Man in Front of the Tree of Life

After God created man, He put man in front of the tree of
life. This shows us very clearly that God wants to dispense
Himself as food for man to receive and enjoy Him. This is why
the Lord Jesus said that He is the living bread from heaven
(John 6:32, 35) and that He came as food to be placed in front
of people for them to receive Him into them as their life.
Recall how one day a Canaanite woman came to beg of the

Lord Jesus, and the Lord said, "It is not good to take the children's bread and throw it to the little dogs" (Matt. 15:25-26). This clearly tells us that the Lord's coming to the earth was His humbling Himself to be a piece of bread and to be placed before men for them to receive. Once a person receives the Lord as bread, then God who is within the Lord enters into him and becomes his life. This is regeneration. Regeneration means that man, in addition to his own life, receives God to be his life. This is man's second life.

The Third Step—
the River of Water of Life Flowing and Watering
to Produce Gold, Bdellium, and Precious Stone

In the third step there is a river flowing and watering. This signifies that from the moment God came into us as life, this life has been moving and flowing in us, watering us like a river. The issue of this moving, flowing, and watering is that pure gold is brought forth. Pure gold symbolizes or denotes the transcendent nature of God. The nature of God is like pure gold. God came into us as life, and this life brought God's nature into us. Peter said that we are "partakers of the divine nature, having escaped the corruption which is in the world by lust" (2 Pet. 1:4). How can we partake of the divine nature? It is through God's entering into us as life. This life moves and flows within us, thus bringing God's nature to us. Hence, we have pure gold within us.

The flowing of the river produces not only gold but also bdellium and precious stone. This indicates that the flowing of God's life in us not only imparts God's nature to us but also causes us to be transformed within. Second Corinthians 3 says that we "are being transformed into the same image from glory to glory, even as from the Lord Spirit" (v. 18). From the day we received God's life and were regenerated, the Spirit of the Lord in us, in coordination with the high pressure and intense heat in the outward environment, has been continually doing this transforming work. Formerly, as earthen men we were lowly vessels—worthless and without honor. However, because God's life has been added into us, we have the element of gold within us. Moreover, because the Holy

Spirit is doing a work of transformation in us, we are being transformed into pearls of great value and precious stones.

The Fourth Step—
Being Built into a Glorious Counterpart

In the fourth step, shown at the end of Genesis 2, the gold, pearl, and precious stones that were produced are collected and built together into a glorious counterpart. In Genesis 2 this counterpart was Eve, who came out of Adam. Adam typifies Christ, who is the unique male in the universe, the unique Bridegroom. Recall that John the Baptist testified that the Lord Jesus, while He was on the earth, was the Bridegroom, the One who had the bride (John 3:29a). As the universal Bridegroom, Christ will gain all those whom He created and redeemed to be His bride. These people whom He created and redeemed are being transformed in His life into precious materials. Furthermore, they are being joined to one another and coordinated together in Him as the Spirit of life to be built up into a mystical man to be His mystical counterpart. This counterpart will be the living image of God to express God in the universe, and it will have the authority of God to represent God on the earth, thereby accomplishing the eternal purpose of God concerning man.

In summary, God created man and put a spirit in man for him to receive God as his life. After God enters into man and becomes his life, He moves and flows in man, causing man to have the element of gold, to be transformed into pearl and precious stone, and eventually to be built together into a corporate man as God's counterpart, having God's image to express God and having God's authority to represent God. This is the vision in the first two chapters of Genesis.

THE GOAL AND THE ACCOMPLISHMENT OF THE VISION

The vision set forth at the beginning of the Bible is like a blueprint at the beginning of a building instruction manual. This vision is a blueprint showing us the work that God intends to do, the goal that He wants to attain, and what He is after in this universe and among men. What He intends to do is to enter into the man He created out of clay that He might be his life. He intends to flow and move in man that man may be transformed to have the pure gold, become pearl and precious stone, and be built together into a mystical entity as His counterpart, having His image and His authority to express Him and represent Him. This is God's blueprint. All of God's work in the universe is to attain this goal.

What a pity, however, that in Genesis 3, before God started to do this work, God's adversary Satan came in the form of a serpent and did a work of interruption. The serpent came in and brought in sin and death. This sin and death defiled and corrupted the man whom God wanted to gain to accomplish His goal. But praise God that although His intention was interrupted, He still intended to accomplish what He had planned. Therefore, when man fell, God came in to promise man that He Himself would come in Christ as the seed of the woman to bruise the head of the serpent and to fulfill righteousness, imparting righteousness to man so that he would have life through righteousness. The seed of the woman would annul the serpent, the righteousness He brought in would replace the sin brought in by the serpent, and the life brought in through Christ would swallow up the death brought in by the serpent. This process started in Genesis 3 and continues until Revelation 20. In Revelation we see that this old serpent will be bound and cast into the lake of fire and that death will also be judged and cast into the lake of fire. Christ will win a complete victory, having dealt with the serpent, sin, death, and all that is in enmity with God. At that time God's work will be completed. The old heaven and the old earth will pass away, and the new heaven and the new earth will arrive. In the new heaven and the new earth the holy city New Jerusalem will appear. The city of the New Jerusalem at the end of the Bible is like a photo of the finished structure on the last page of a building instruction manual. If we compare this picture of the finished structure with the blueprint at the beginning of the manual, we will see that the two match each other and are exactly alike. In other words, if we compare the record of the last two chapters of Revelation with that of the first two chapters of Genesis, we will see that they are exactly the same.

THE NEW JERUSALEM
BEING THE WIFE OF THE LAMB

We must especially notice that the city of the New Jerusalem is not a matter of a place, because this city is actually the bride, the wife of the Lamb. Once some friends who were speaking with me concerning the New Jerusalem strongly suggested that the New Jerusalem was a place. I merely smiled and said, "No one would be so foolish as to want to marry a place as a wife." Please remember that the New Jerusalem is not a place but a corporate great man. In what way is the New Jerusalem a corporate entity? In the city, the twelve gates are the twelve tribes of the children of Israel, and the twelve foundations are the twelve apostles of the Lamb. The twelve tribes represent all the redeemed saints of God in the Old Testament, and the twelve apostles represent all the saved ones in the New Testament. These two groups include all the redeemed and saved persons among the Jews and the Gentiles in both the Old Testament and the New Testament. We must realize that the record of the New Jerusalem is figurative. It uses a picture to show us the meaning of the New Jerusalem. Hence, when we read this portion, we have to read it as if we were looking at a picture, and we must try our best to understand its meaning. This picture describes all the redeemed people throughout the generations, including the saints in the Old Testament and all the saved ones in the New Testament, who have been gathered together to form the city of the New Jerusalem. This city is a living, mystical entity. It is the bride of the Lamb, the corporate counterpart that Christ wants to obtain. Therefore, it is definitely not a place but a person.

We have already said that John the Baptist testified of the Lord Jesus, referring to Him as the Lamb on the one hand and as the Bridegroom on the other. Indeed, Christ is the universal Bridegroom, and all the redeemed people of God are collectively the universal bride. The heavens and the earth are like the wedding chamber. God in His Son, Christ, was incarnated. He became a man and passed through death and resurrection to be the universal Bridegroom to marry all those whom He has redeemed throughout the generations. The totality of all these redeemed ones is the universal bride.

In the first two chapters of Genesis we see that a part of Adam was taken out to become Adam's counterpart, who was Eve. In Ephesians 5 the apostle Paul tells us that this picture typifies the relationship between Christ and the church. While Adam was sleeping, his side was broken open, and a rib was taken out of him. Likewise, when Christ was crucified, His side was also broken open, and something flowed out of His side. The bone that was taken from Adam's side became Eve as the counterpart of Adam, and the water and blood that flowed from Christ's side accomplished redemption and imparted life to us, thereby producing the church. Therefore, just as Eve came out from Adam, so also the church came out of Christ, and just as Eve returned to Adam and became one flesh with Adam, so also the church was given back to Christ and became one with Christ. This is what the apostle Paul tells us in Ephesians 5, saying, "The two shall be one flesh. This mystery is great, but I speak with regard to Christ and the church" (vv. 31b-32). Therefore, the church is the universal counterpart of Christ, and this is signified by the city of the New Jerusalem, which is ultimately manifested at the end of the Scriptures. Therefore, God's work throughout the ages will be finished and accomplished in the New Jerusalem.

SPECIAL FEATURES OF THE NEW JERUSALEM

Now we want to briefly look at the features of the New Jerusalem that through this we may know how the church is built and what the building of the church is.

God Being the Life Therein

First, we have to see that in Genesis 2 the tree of life was outside the corporate great man. If we have the insight, we will see that the Adam who stood in front of the tree of life on that day represented not only himself alone but also all of his descendants throughout the ages. Therefore, that Adam was a corporate great man, and outside of that great man was the tree of life. However, we see in the New Jerusalem, which is the composition of all of the redeemed ones throughout the ages as a corporate great man, that the tree of life has already entered into this man. Therefore, this picture shows us that the God who was outside of man in Genesis 2, has now entered into man and has been mingled with man. He has become the life of man, living within man. Moreover, this God also flows in man as living water to water man, and He is also in man as the fruit of the tree of life to supply and nourish man.

In order to have the real building, the church must have God as her life to flow, water, and supply her. We often say that when a certain church is blessed, she is full of life. To be full of life is to be full of God. In such a church God in Christ is flowing and watering as the river of water of life, and He is also supplying and nourishing as the tree of life. In this way all those who are in the church can drink the water of life and eat the fruit of the tree of life. Only at this point can the church have the real building. In the first two chapters of Genesis the tree of life had not yet entered into man. Therefore, there was no building at that point. But in the last two chapters of Revelation, in the New Jerusalem, the tree of life has already entered into man. Therefore, all the saints can be built together into a structure as a corporate entity.

Having the Throne of God

Second, in this city of the New Jerusalem, the corporate great man, there is the throne of God. The river of water of life proceeds out of the throne of God, and the tree of life grows on both sides of the river. The meaning of this picture is that within this corporate man there must be the reigning of God; that is, God must be on the throne. When God reigns, His life will flow out of the reigning. Therefore, please remember that although there may be confusion and lawlessness everywhere else, in the church built by God everything must be absolutely in order, because the throne of God is here and God's authority is here.

In this age when you go and look at the societies among the human race, it is difficult to find one that is not in confusion. Almost all of them are full of opinions, criticism, judging, and attacking. However, please remember that although this may be acceptable in human society, it cannot be so in the church. If there is quarreling, opinions, gossip, criticism, judging, and attacking in a local church, then you know that that church has lost the nature of building, since she has lost the throne of God and the authority of God. If we want God to have the building in the church, then there must be the throne of God in the church. Only when we have God's authority with everything under the ruling of God and everything in perfect order will the life of God be able to flow and to supply.

God and the Lamb Being the Temple of the City

Third, this city, New Jerusalem, is different from the city of Jerusalem in the Old Testament. In the Old Testament there was a temple in the city, but in the New Jerusalem there is no temple, because God and the Lamb are the temple of the city. This shows us that this city is full of the presence of God and of the Lamb. The presence of God and of the Lamb is the temple of this city. In the same way, whenever someone comes into a church that has been built up, he cannot but bow his head and worship, saying, "God is here. This place is full of the presence of God." Such a church does not merely have some religious rituals and a meeting hall. Instead, what people meet is God Himself, and what they touch is Christ Himself. The presence of God and of Christ becomes the temple, the center of man's worship.

CHAPTER THREE

THE BUILDING OF
THE TABERNACLE AND THE TEMPLE BEING
THE CENTER OF THE OLD TESTAMENT

Scripture Reading: Exo. 27:1-2, 9-10, 17-19; 38:8; Num. 16:37-40;
Exo. 25:10-11, 23-24, 31; 26:15-19, 26-29; 30:1-3

In the first two messages we briefly looked at the revelation at the beginning and at the end of the Scriptures. We pointed out that both at the beginning and at the end of the Bible, the central revelation is the mystical building. In other words, God's intention as revealed in the Scriptures is to build a dwelling place for Himself and a Body for His Son, Christ. This dwelling place or Body is His mystical counterpart in the universe. Neither the dwelling place, the Body, nor the counterpart is composed of a single individual. Rather, each is the aggregate of a great number of people as one corporate entity. This corporate entity as the corporate great man is composed of all the saved ones throughout the ages who have been gradually transformed in the eternal life of God and who have been built up together. This corporate great man is the dwelling place of God, the Body of Christ, and the mystical counterpart of God in the universe. I trust that you are clear about these matters. Beginning from this message, we will look at the long, middle section of the Bible from Genesis 3 to Revelation 20. Due to the limitation of time we will look only at the main points briefly.

THE TABERNACLE AND THE TEMPLE BEING
THE CENTER OF THE OLD TESTAMENT

If we would carefully read through the whole Bible and look at it with a bird's-eye view, we would discover that the entire Old Testament is centered on the tabernacle and the temple. In fact, we may say that the entire Old Testament is a history of the tabernacle and the temple. With the exception of a small section at the beginning of Genesis, the thirty-nine books of the Old Testament, from the story of Abraham's calling in Genesis 12 to the end of Malachi, are concerned mainly with the history of the people of Israel, which was clearly centered on the tabernacle and the temple. The tabernacle and the temple were the most central issue to the children of Israel. When their condition was good, the condition of the tabernacle was also good. When their condition was not good, the condition of the tabernacle was not good either. When their relationship with God was normal, God could dwell in the tabernacle. When there was a problem between them and God, God would leave the tabernacle. In principle, it was the same with the temple.

We know that the tabernacle and the temple are in reality the same one entity in two stages and that this one entity is God's dwelling place or house. The difference is that the tabernacle was God's movable dwelling place, and the temple was God's fixed dwelling place. The tabernacle was the temple's predecessor, and the temple was the tabernacle's successor. When the people of God were wandering in the wilderness, their center was the tabernacle. After the people of God entered into Canaan and dwelt in the promised good land, their center was the temple. Therefore, the tabernacle and the temple are actually one in significance, function, and typology. Both were the dwelling place of God.

Not only so, in the original language of the Old Testament, both the tabernacle and the temple were called the house of God. This also proves that the tabernacle and the temple were actually one entity denoting the house of God.

THE TABERNACLE AND THE TEMPLE BEING A STORY OF BUILDING

What is the story of the tabernacle and the temple? Simply speaking, it is a story of building. After the Israelites held the Passover, left Egypt, crossed the Red Sea, and arrived at Mount Sinai and after they received the law of God and saw the heavenly pattern, the one thing they did together with one mind and with a united effort was to build the tabernacle. Among the children of Israel were men who worked in wood, bronze, silver, and gold, as well as weavers. They all worked in cooperation to build the tabernacle. On the first day of the first month of the second year, at the commencement of a new year, they raised up the tabernacle according to the command of God. At that time, the glory of God filled the tabernacle, and God Himself came to dwell among them. From that day on, God had a dwelling place or habitation on the earth, and He dwelt among the children of Israel.

The book of Numbers clearly tells us that the journey of the children of Israel in the wilderness was centered on the tabernacle. When they encamped, the twelve tribes encamped on the four sides of the tabernacle, three tribes on each side. This was a miniature of the New Jerusalem. We all know that the New Jerusalem is the tabernacle of God among men. It has four sides—east, west, north, and south—and on each side are three gates on which the names of the twelve tribes of Israel are inscribed. This is exactly like the situation of the children of Israel when they encamped around the tabernacle. Therefore, do not think that the situation of the New Jerusalem will be brought in only at the time of the new heaven and new earth. No, a rough model of this situation was already in existence when the tabernacle was raised up at the foot of Mount Sinai. What were the children of Israel doing in the wilderness? They were doing nothing but ministering to the tabernacle. When they encamped, they raised up the tabernacle, and the twelve tribes offered sacrifices and worshipped around the tabernacle. When the cloud was taken up, they dismantled the tabernacle and carried it with them as they went forward. When the cloud settled down again, they raised up the tabernacle again. What the Israelites did in the wilderness for forty years was actually the story of the tabernacle.

We have to see the vision that there was a tabernacle among the children of Israel, that the history of Israel depended on this tabernacle, and that everything they did was for this tabernacle. Even the warfare that they fought when they entered Canaan was for this tabernacle. The warfare reveals that God wanted to have a piece of land upon which He could securely set up His dwelling place on the earth. Therefore, after the children of Israel crossed the Jordan, they conquered city after city and occupied place after place. Before they possessed the whole land of Canaan, God told them to set up the tabernacle in Shiloh. In this way the tabernacle temporarily settled down until the ark was taken captive.

Afterward, David moved the ark into the city of David and set it in the tent that he had pitched. Later, he intended to build a temple for Jehovah. Through the prophet Nathan, God told him, "I will appoint a place for My people Israel and will plant them there, that they may dwell in their own place and be disturbed no more; and the sons of wickedness will ill-treat them no more as before" (2 Sam. 7:10). Moreover, God declared that He would make David a house, that He would raise up his seed to sit on the throne after him, and that it was his seed who would build a house for His name (vv. 11b-13). Since God delighted in this matter, the building of the temple was completed during the reign of Solomon. However, not long after the temple was built, Israel became desolate. The temple was torn down by the Babylonians, and Jerusalem was destroyed. After the seventy years of captivity were fulfilled, the children of Israel returned to their own land group by group, and they started to restore the city and rebuild the temple. While they were restoring the city, they worked with one hand and held a weapon with the other (Neh. 4:17). This shows us that building requires fighting. This takes us to the end of Malachi, the last book of the Old Testament. Now that we have pointed out these matters in such a simple way, it is very clear that the history of the Old Testament is a history of the tabernacle and the temple, a history of building.

THE LORD JESUS BEING
GOD'S TABERNACLE AND GOD'S TEMPLE

Now let us look at the New Testament. The first great matter in the New Testament is the Lord's incarnation in Bethlehem. Incarnation is God entering into man, God putting on humanity. John 1:14 says that the Word became flesh and tabernacled among men. Originally, God dwelt in the heavens, but when He was born in Bethlehem, He came to put on flesh and to be among men. The flesh that He put on was a tabernacle in which He dwelt. Therefore, His incarnation was His tabernacling among men, and His body was the tabernacle that God had raised up among men.

In John 2, the Lord said to the Jews, "Destroy this temple, and in three days I will raise it up" (v. 19). We all know that the temple which the Lord mentions here denotes His own body. Therefore, in His incarnation the Lord was a tabernacle and a temple, which are actually the same thing. Therefore, the Lord Jesus in the four Gospels was the temple of God among men, and God dwelt in this temple. Jesus the Nazarene is not only our Savior, the Lamb of God, and the Bridegroom who will take the bride, He is also the temple, the dwelling place, the tabernacle of God among men. God dwelt in Him as the living tabernacle, the living temple. The Jews, who were utilized by the devil, hated the Lord Jesus and crucified Him, thus destroying Him as the temple. However, after three days He was resurrected from the dead, and He released His life to regenerate us. As a result, in His resurrection many people were built together to become the enlarged temple, which is the church.

THE CHURCH ALSO BEING THE TEMPLE OF GOD

Now let us look at the book of Acts and the Epistles. The subject of this section from Acts 2 to the end of Revelation is the church as the temple. In 1 Corinthians 3 the apostle Paul told the Corinthian believers that they were God's temple (v. 16) and God's building (v. 9b) and that the apostles were God's fellow workers for God's building (v. 9a). Moreover, he said, "As a wise master builder I have laid a foundation, and another builds upon it. But let each man take heed how he builds upon it" (v. 10). Are we building with wood, grass, and stubble or with gold, silver, and precious stones? In Ephesians 2 Paul says, "So then you are no longer strangers and sojourners, but you are fellow citizens with the saints and members of the household of God, being built...into a holy temple in the Lord...into a dwelling place of God in spirit" (vv. 19-22). Likewise, Peter says, "Coming to Him, a living stone,...you yourselves also, as living stones, are being built up as a spiritual house" (1 Pet. 2:4-5a).

Therefore, the whole New Testament is also a story of the temple. The Lord Jesus is a temple, and the church is also a temple. The Lord Jesus as the Head with the church as the Body form a complete temple. At the end of the Bible, a big structure appears—the holy city New Jerusalem.

THE THREAD OF LIFE AND BUILDING RUNNING THROUGH THE ENTIRE BIBLE

The more you read the Bible, the more you will have the impression that the central subject of the Scriptures is that God in Christ came to be life to us that we may be built up as His dwelling place. Both the types of the Old Testament and the plain words of the New Testament speak of this same matter. What a pity that very few in the church today have seen this, and even fewer speak about this. According to my own experience, ever since I was very young, I attended Sunday school where I listened to people telling Bible stories and ministers preaching sermons. I often heard people talking about how Adam had sinned by eating the fruit that had been forbidden by God, but I never heard that the tree of life denotes God Himself and that God wants man to eat Him to receive Him as life. For about four and a half years after I was saved, I heard more than a thousand messages in a certain Christian group, yet I never heard a message which said that the tree of life in Genesis 2 signifies that God wants to enter into man in the form of food that man may have Him as life. Thank the Lord that over ten years after I was saved, I heard from a servant of God that the purpose of God is that He wants to enter into man to be man's life and that this is why after creating man He put man in front of the tree of life. He wanted man to face the tree of life and to eat the fruit of the tree of life. Since that day I have been inwardly enlightened to see that God's relationship with me is a relationship of life.

However, God's purpose does not stop there. After speaking about the tree of life, Genesis 2 also mentions that there is a river, and wherever its water flows, there is gold, bdellium, and precious stone. Then in Exodus, when the children of Israel were building the tabernacle in the wilderness, the principal material they used was gold. For example, the lampstand was made of pure gold, and the ark, the incense altar, the showbread table, and the boards were made of wood overlaid with gold. Moreover, the garment worn by the high priest had a breastplate and shoulder pieces, which had precious stones enclosed in settings of gold. Besides these, the chains were a twisted cordage work of pure gold. The shoulder pieces were woven with gold, blue, purple, and scarlet strands. Therefore, when the tabernacle was raised up and the high priest, wearing the holy garment, went in to minister, the situation inside was entirely of gold and precious stones. If you read all of this, eventually you will see that the gold and precious stones are not for anything else but for the building of God's dwelling place.

When we read the story of how Solomon built the temple, we see again that everything inside the temple was overlaid with gold and that the outside of the temple was covered with large and precious stones. You can imagine the situation when the high priest, wearing the holy garments and the ephod with the shoulder pieces and the breastplate, went into the temple to minister. Outside the temple were precious stones, and inside was the gold; the high priest was standing in the temple in the middle of all the gold and precious stones. Now we can see that the pure gold and the precious stones are for the building of God.

As we read on, we come to the New Testament. In his first Epistle to the church in Corinth, the apostle Paul said, "We are God's fellow workers; you are...God's building" (3:9). Furthermore, he said, "According to the grace of God given to me, as a wise master builder I have laid a foundation, and another builds upon it. But let each man take heed how he builds upon it" (v. 10). Then Paul went on to say that they should not build with wood, grass, and stubble but with gold, silver, and precious stones. At this point we should be even more clear that gold and precious stones are altogether materials for building God's dwelling place. As we read on and come to the end of the Bible, we see a city of pure gold, like clear glass. Its wall is built with jasper, and its gates are pearls. At this point we should be absolutely clear that the gold, pearl, and precious stones mentioned in Genesis 2 are altogether for the building of God's dwelling place!

I would like to tell you that the Bible is a book on building. The entire Bible shows how we human beings who are made of clay have received God as our life and are thereby being transformed within. God as our life is like living water flowing within us. The result is that we who are made of clay are being transformed into gold, pearl, and precious stones and are being built together into the dwelling place of God. This is the Bible's focus from the beginning to the end. I say again that the Bible is a book on building. At the beginning it shows us some scattered materials, and at the end it shows us a completed building. At the beginning it shows us three kinds of precious materials—gold, pearl, and precious stones, and at the end we see that these three kinds of precious materials have been built into a city of glory and splendor.

THE REVELATION OF BETHEL

Let us now look at the story of God's building of the tabernacle in the Old Testament. However, before looking at the tabernacle I would like to speak a word to lay a foundation.

In the Old Testament we see that God chose some of the forefathers such as Enosh, Enoch, Noah, Abraham, Isaac, and Jacob. Jacob was the last among the forefathers whom God chose. Out from Jacob came the twelve tribes, the Israelites. We all know the story of Jacob. Jacob was a person who grasped, struggled, and supplanted. When he was in his mother's womb, he struggled with his brother Esau to get out first, but he failed. Then he used his craftiness to seize the birthright with its blessings. Consequently, his brother Esau wanted to kill him, so his mother told him to flee to Haran. As Jacob went out from Beer-sheba toward Haran, he came to a certain place and spent the night there because the sun had set. He took one of the stones of that place, made it his pillow, and lay down to sleep. Then a marvelous thing happened—he had a dream. In this dream there was a ladder set up on the earth, its top reaching to heaven, and the angels of God were ascending and descending on it. Furthermore, Jehovah was standing above it, and He spoke to him, promising to give him and his descendants the land on which he lay. After Jacob awoke from his sleep, he said, "How awesome is this place! This is none other than the house of God, and this is the gate of heaven." Then he rose up early in the morning and took the stone that he had put under his head, and he set it up as a pillar and poured oil on top of it. He called the name of that place Bethel, which means the house of God. Then Jacob made a business deal with the Lord, saying, "If God will be with me and will keep me in this way that I go and will give me bread to eat and garments to put on, so that I return to my father's house in peace, then Jehovah will be my God, and this stone, which I have set up as a pillar, will be God's house" (Gen. 28:10-22).

I would like you all to take note that this is the first time that the house of God is mentioned in the Bible, and in this revelation we see that the house of God comes from the oil poured upon the stone. Most readers of the Bible know that oil in the holy Scriptures denotes the Holy Spirit who is God coming forth to reach and enter into man. The stone denotes a saved person. Previously, we were pieces of clay, but after we were saved, we were transformed into stones. When Peter confessed to the Lord Jesus, "You are the Christ," the Lord immediately said to him, "You are Peter [or, a stone]" (Matt. 16:16, 18). Therefore, the pouring of the oil upon the stone indicates the mingling together of God and the saved ones, and this mingling becomes the house of God. Therefore, a principle of primary importance concerning the building of God is the mingling of God with man.

When God revealed this vision to Jacob, He promised Jacob that He would give the land on which Jacob lay, which was the land of Canaan, to him and to his seed. God also promised Jacob that his seed would be as the dust of the earth (Gen. 28:13-14). We all know that the seed of Jacob later became the house of Israel, which was the house of God.

Here we again touch the story of building. In Genesis 2 we see that the flow of the water of life produces gold, bdellium, and precious stones as materials for the building. Then in chapter twenty-eight we see oil being poured upon a stone, issuing in the house of God. In these passages we see the story of building. We see the stones as the materials for building, the pouring of the oil upon the stones as the way of building, and the house of God as the result. At this point, the vision of building is clear enough—God uses the way of pouring the oil upon the stone to build His house on the earth.

Jacob stayed in his uncle Laban's home for twenty years and then returned from Paddan-aram and dwelt in Shechem (33:18). One day God came again to Jacob and said, "Rise up, go up to Bethel, and dwell there" (35:1). God was calling Jacob to go back to the place where God had appeared to him when he was fleeing from his brother. In other words, God was calling him to return to God's house. Subsequently, Jacob and his household went down to Egypt and dwelt in Egypt until Moses was raised up by God to lead the Israelites out of Egypt. When the Israelites came to the foot of Mount Sinai, God wanted them to build a tabernacle to be His dwelling place on earth. We know that this tabernacle was only a type. In reality, the children of Israel themselves were the house of God.

From this point onward the story of building is completely made manifest. God had a group of people on the earth who were coordinated, knit, and built together to be the dwelling place of God. Therefore, when the tabernacle was raised up, God's glory filled the tabernacle. God's glory filled the midst of the children of Israel, and therefore, God could dwell among them.

SATAN'S FRUSTRATION AND COUNTERFEITS

Now let us go back and look at some matters on the negative side. Most readers of the Bible know that after God's purpose and the way to fulfill it were revealed in the first two chapters of Genesis, the serpent, who was the incarnation of Satan, appeared in chapter three. Satan came to harm and damage man by injecting his poison—sin—into man, thus bringing man into death. If we have the light concerning building, we will see that the reason Satan wanted to ruin man and put man to death was that he wanted to frustrate God's building. The man created by God was God's material for building. Therefore, in his stratagem to frustrate God's building, Satan's first step was to poison the material for the building.

Satan not only used subtlety to poison the material prepared by God for His building, but he also preceded God by producing a counterfeit that was according to what God had wanted to produce. Satan knew that what God ultimately wanted was a builded city, so before God could do that, Satan did something to produce a counterfeit. God wanted to build a city, so Satan stirred up some persons whom he had poisoned to build another city. Hence, in Genesis 4 Cain built a city, and he named the city after the name of his son, Enoch. That city was full of sin and wickedness. What kind of image did the city of Enoch have? What did it express? No doubt, the city of Enoch altogether had the image of Satan and completely expressed Satan. The city of Enoch was a mixture of Satan and man.

Gradually, the wickedness of this city became so great that it incurred God's judgment by the flood. We must remember that the age which was destroyed by the flood had the city of Enoch as its center. God saved Noah and his household from that destruction, and Noah's building of the ark was again a story of building. Not long afterward, Satan came again to corrupt the descendants of Noah, and he instigated them to build Babel. They wanted to build a city and a tower with its top reaching heaven so that they might make a name for themselves. Their rebellion directly touched the realm of heaven. Therefore, God Himself intervened and stopped their rebellion.

After judging Babel, God called out from Babel a person named Abraham. God promised Abraham to give him and his seed the land of Canaan. Moreover, God also promised to make Abraham into a great nation. Therefore, Abraham pitched a tent and built an altar in Canaan (12:7-8). I want you to see that the one matter emphasized in the entire Bible is the matter of building. The people utilized by Satan were building something, and Abraham, who had been called out by God, was also building something. Abraham's whole life was a story of pitching his tent and building an altar in the land of Canaan. The tent that he pitched and the altar that he built were just a miniature or scaled-down model of the tabernacle built by his descendants in the wilderness.

On the other hand, Lot, Abraham's companion, went down to another city, the third corrupt city recorded in the Bible. The first corrupt city was the city of Enoch, which was destroyed by the flood. The second was Babel, which was judged by God. The third was the city of Sodom, where Lot went. Sodom was also a building constructed with the mixture of Satan and man, and Lot fell into its midst. Eventually, Sodom suffered God's judgment and was destroyed by fire. Only Abraham was still dwelling in a tent, building an altar, and serving God in the land of Canaan.

Subsequently, the descendants of Abraham went down to Egypt. At that time the fourth city that Satan built appeared. This city comprised the two storage cities that the Israelites built for Pharaoh when they were serving as slaves in Egypt. Pharaoh forced them to build these two cities with bricks of baked clay. One day, however, God delivered the Israelites out of Egypt so that they no longer had to bake clay into bricks to build cities for Pharaoh. Instead, they refined gold and silver to build God's tabernacle.

When the children of Israel entered into Canaan, they rose up to build the city of Jerusalem and the temple. In contrast, Satan also built something; he built the city of Babylon. At the end of the Bible, we not only see the New Jerusalem as the consummation of God's building throughout the ages, but we also see the great Babylon as the consummation of Satan's building throughout the ages. These two cities are in contrast with one another. We all know that it was the armies of Babylon that destroyed the city of Jerusalem and the temple and carried away the vessels that were in the temple to Babylon. When the children of Israel were restored, they came back from Babylon. Ezra said that on the first day of the first month of the year he began to go up from Babylon to return to Jerusalem (Ezra 7:9). Babylon represents Satan's building, and Jerusalem represents the building of God. The two are in contrast with one another from the beginning to the end of the Bible. Therefore, the entire Bible speaks of the matter of building, both on the positive side and on the negative side. Satan wants to utilize man to build the great Babylon, while God wants to gain a group of people to build the New Jerusalem. We can clearly see these two lines in the Bible.

THE BUILDING OF THE TABERNACLE

Now let us look at the building of the tabernacle. After the children of Israel held the Passover, applied the blood of the lamb, ate the flesh of the lamb, left Egypt, crossed the Red Sea, were instructed by God at the foot of Mount Sinai, and received the pattern on the mountain, they rose up to build the tabernacle to be the dwelling place of God.

Most Bible readers acknowledge that it is not easy to study the type of the tabernacle. I would like to tell you that if we want to understand the tabernacle, we must read the Bible with the matter of building in view, because the tabernacle is essentially a story of building. On the perimeter of the tabernacle were the hangings, which were like an enclosing wall, and within these hangings was the outer court. In the midst of the outer court was the tent, the dwelling place of God. This was altogether a building. Whenever a person entered the tabernacle, the first item he met in the outer court was the bronze altar, upon which all the sacrifices to God were offered. Proceeding a little farther, he came to the bronze laver, where everyone who came to minister before God first washed his hands and feet, purging away all the defilement of the earth. Then a little farther on was the tent, within which were four items. The innermost item was the Ark, which was also called the Ark of the Testimony because it contained the two tablets of the testimony (Exo. 25:16, 21). Outside the Ark on the north side of the tent was the showbread table upon which the bread was continually set. On the south side opposite the table was the golden lampstand whose lamps shone continually. In front of the Ark and between the showbread table and the lampstand was the golden incense altar upon which the priest burned fragrant incense to God. These four items and all the boards inside the tabernacle were either overlaid with gold or were completely made of pure gold. The tabernacle was entirely a matter of gold. Therefore, whenever a person entered the tabernacle, all he saw was pure gold. This picture altogether depicts the building.

Now let us look at the tabernacle and its furniture according to the order shown in the Bible. The record of the tabernacle in Exodus first mentions the altar and the laver and then speaks about the hangings of the outer court. The spiritual meaning of this is that in God's building there is first the altar, and then from the altar the hangings are produced. In the same principle, the four pieces of furniture within the tent are mentioned first, and then out of these four items the tent is produced. This is very clear from the record of Exodus. The spiritual meaning of this is quite rich. Hence, we need to look at these items one by one according to their order of spiritual significance.

THE MEANING OF THE ALTAR

In this message we will examine only the first item in this picture of the building. In this building the first item according to our experience is the bronze altar. The altar is the only way that man can come near to God. Man can fellowship with God only through the offerings on the bronze altar. The meanings hidden in this picture are too numerous. We will look briefly only at three aspects of the altar.

The first meaning of the altar is judgment. Since man has been damaged by Satan and has the poison of sin, sin must first be dealt with in order for man to draw near to God. There is no other way to deal with sin but to pass through judgment. Therefore, at the altar there is a fire to burn all the offerings. Furthermore, the altar is overlaid with bronze, and this bronze came from the censers that were held in the hands of the two hundred fifty rebellious people. They were judged by fire, and God commanded that their censers be taken out of the fire and be beaten into plates for a covering for the altar (Num. 16:37-40). Therefore, bronze signifies God's judgment.

The second meaning of the altar is redemption. Whenever God judged the sacrifice offered on the altar and burned it with fire, redemption was accomplished. Thus, anyone who passes through God's judgment at the altar is also redeemed by God.

The third meaning of the altar is consecration. Everyone who has been redeemed by God must ultimately be put on the altar and offered to God as a burnt offering.

This is the way the building of God begins in us who were sinners poisoned by Satan. If we want to be built by God to be His dwelling place, then we must begin by being judged. This is why the Lord said that when the Holy Spirit comes, "He will convict the world concerning sin and concerning righteousness and concerning judgment" (John 16:8). God has already judged our sins on the cross, so we must also judge ourselves in the light of this judgment. Our living must be judged, our clothing must be judged, our family must be judged, and our career must be judged. Everything that is ours must pass through the judgment. This is in contrast to the praise and flattery in human society. The first sentence that the church of God must tell someone who comes to listen to the gospel is, "Dear friend, you are a sinner!" Many people cannot take this, for they consider this as a rebuke. However, if you and I are not sinners, then what are we? Therefore, if we want to be built, the first thing that we must do is that we must condemn ourselves. What we are, what we have, and what we do, whether they are good or bad, all have to be put on the cross, pass through the burning, and be put to death.

All those who have not passed through this kind of judgment and have not been judged at the bronze altar cannot be redeemed. All those who have passed through the judgment have been cleansed by the blood and have been redeemed. All those who have been redeemed are required by God to consecrate themselves to be offered as burnt offerings. Therefore, the altar of redemption becomes the altar of burnt offering. Everything that is placed on the altar is completely gained by God. If you are not completely gained by God, you cannot be built by God. To be gained by God, you must first judge yourself, second, you must be redeemed, and third, you must offer yourself completely to God, allowing God to gain you as material for the building. Remember that the building of God starts at the altar; blessed is he who starts here!

CHAPTER FOUR

THE BUILDING OF THE TABERNACLE

Scripture Reading: Exo. 40:17-35

We have already briefly looked at the meaning of the altar. If we want to be built by God into His dwelling place, then all we are, all we have, and all we can do must be judged before God. Thank God that this judgment has already been accomplished on the cross of the Lord. Through His death on the cross the Lord has already judged everything. If we receive His all-inclusive death, we will not only pass through the judgment, but we will also be redeemed. After we are redeemed through His judgment, we must offer our everything to God. We must commit ourselves completely into the Lord's hand, acknowledging that He has absolute authority over us so that He may gain us completely. This is the first step of our being built. If a person wants to be built by God as material for His dwelling place, the first step he must take is to pass through judgment, redemption, and consecration at the cross.

THE EXPERIENCE OF THE LAVER

As we go on from the altar, we come to the laver. The laver was made completely of bronze. Therefore, most Bible readers acknowledge that from a spiritual point of view, the laver comes from the bronze altar. The altar was overlaid with bronze, and the laver was also made of bronze. However, the bronze of the altar was a little different from the bronze of the laver. The altar was covered with the bronze plates beaten out of the censers carried by the two hundred fifty rebels who were judged by fire (Num. 16:38-40). The laver, however, was made of the bronze from the mirrors of the women who served at the entrance of the tabernacle (Exo. 38:8). At that time there was no such thing as glass, so women used polished, shining brass as mirrors. Therefore, the laver does not denote judgment. Instead, it denotes the Holy Spirit's enlightening of us. According to Titus 3:5, the laver denotes the renewing work of the Holy Spirit upon us.

After we are redeemed by the Lord and consecrate ourselves to Him, the Holy Spirit as light continually shines on us, causing us to sense that we were wrong or defiled in certain matters or that we have sinned against God or are unable to present ourselves before God in other matters. This kind of reproving by the Holy Spirit is based upon what the Lord accomplished on the cross. The Holy Spirit may show us a certain matter and say to us, "Since such a matter, action, and living has already been judged by the Lord on the cross, why is it that it is still in you today?" After we receive this kind of enlightening and reproving and seek for cleansing, then the Holy Spirit does the work of washing and renewing in us, completely purging us of all the filthy and improper situations. This is our experience of the washing at the laver. Our being purified is the second step of our being built.

THE HANGINGS AS THE BOUNDARY

The result of the work of the two preceding steps is the producing of the hangings of the court. We all know that the hangings formed the boundary of the outer court, which may also be considered the boundary of God's building. If a person wants to be built by God, to have a part in God's house, and to serve God together with all the children of God, then he must be within this boundary. In other words, there must be a boundary in his daily living and walk. The hangings were made of fine white linen, and the sockets for the pillars were made of bronze. On the pillars were the silver hooks and the silver connecting rods which joined the pillars together (Exo. 27:10). Now let us look at these items one by one.

The Bronze Sockets

The bronze sockets were the bases for the hangings of the court. Hence, they formed the foundation of the boundary.

Spiritually speaking, the experience of the bronze sockets is produced through the experience of the bronze altar. The boundary of our being built before God is based on our having been judged before God. If we want to be built in the church, then we and all that we have must sooner or later pass through God's judgment. Perhaps when we were first saved, we only saw that the Lord had judged our sins on the cross. Gradually, however, the Lord will show us that not only were our sins judged by God on the cross, but even we ourselves, including all that we are, all that we have, and all that we can do, were judged by God on the cross. Once we see this under the shining of the Holy Spirit, our entire living and walk will be spontaneously and severely judged under the light of the cross. It is only after such a judging that we have the foundation for the building, the bronze sockets of the hangings of the court.

If a saved one does not abandon himself to a carefree living but is willing to be built together in the church and to coordinate and serve together with the saints, then he will not escape this kind of judgment. The Holy Spirit will surely work in him to bring his entire being into the light to show him that everything of himself has to be judged and has already been judged on the cross. Then he should follow the Holy Spirit to deal with and condemn these matters one by one before God, based on the judgment that the Lord received on the cross. In this way he will establish the boundary of his service before God.

The Silver Rods and the Silver Hooks

Let us look at the silver rods and the silver hooks of the pillars. No doubt these items denote redemption, because the people of Israel gave this silver for the redemption of their lives. The meaning of the silver rods and the silver hooks being on the pillars which rested upon the bronze sockets is that whatever passes through God's judgment receives God's redemption. The degree of God's judgment determines the degree of man's redemption. Is this not so in our experience? In our living and our career, whatever is judged is redeemed and accepted by God.

The Hangings of Fine White Linen

Now let us look at the hangings on the silver hooks. The hangings of the outer court were made of fine white linen. In typology, fine white linen signifies the righteous and pure conduct of man before God. A person who has passed through the cross and the washing and renewing of the Holy Spirit has the white linen hangings upon him. Because his conduct is pure and white before man and God, a boundary or separating line has been established in his living. When people observe him, they have to admit that he is clearly separated from the world. The world is a mess, and the people of the world are in filthiness, but this person who has been rescued by God and is being built by God has a boundary upon him which distinctly separates him from the world. Because everything of himself has passed through God's judgment, has received God's redemption, and has been cleansed by the Holy Spirit, his living and walk have become a boundary line that separates him from the world.

Up to this point, everything has been a matter of outward conduct and not a matter of inward nature. At this stage, although this person has been judged, redeemed, and washed to be pure and white before man and God, he has only gone through an outward change in behavior and has not necessarily had much transformation in life. He may not have a great deal of the expression of the divine life and nature as gold in him. Therefore, according to the picture of the building, he still has to enter further.

THE EXPERIENCE OF THE TABERNACLE

Now let us look at the items inside the tabernacle. We all know that being a Christian is not merely a matter of our outward living and walk but even more a matter of our inward life and nature. Therefore, merely having the fine white linen hangings on the outside is not enough. The life within as gold must be expressed. In the outer court, you see only the bronze, silver, and white fine linen but not the gold. Therefore, as a saved one grows in his spiritual life, he will gradually turn from the outside to the inside. This is according to what we often say about turning within. We cannot merely be good Christians, well-behaved Christians, cleansed Christians, or faultless Christians in an outward way. We cannot merely be Christians in the outer court. Rather, we must enter the tabernacle and be Christians in the Holy Place.

We have already said that when you entered the tabernacle, that is, the Holy Place and the Holy of Holies, everything you saw was of gold. The tabernacle's four sides were boards overlaid with gold, and the furniture within it was either made of pure, solid gold or was overlaid with gold. Although the bases of the tabernacle were made of silver and the curtains were of fine twined linen and blue and purple and scarlet strands, the important component within the tabernacle was pure gold. The spiritual meaning of this is that when we advance in our experience from the outer court into the Holy Place, we will discover that within us is pure gold, which is God in Christ as our life. Therefore, we will learn to live not outwardly but inwardly, paying attention not only to the boundary line of fine white linen without but also to the life of the gold within. From that time onward we will know how to contact the Christ within, touch the feeling within, and have fellowship with the Lord within, inquiring of Him and looking to Him. This is the experience of dealing with the life of the gold within.

The Testimony of the Ark

Concerning the items within the tabernacle, we have to start from the Ark. The Ark is sometimes called the Ark of the Testimony, because hidden within it were the tablets of the covenant that God made with the children of Israel. The law that was written on the tablets was on the one hand a covenant and on the other hand a testimony, the testimony of God. Therefore, the Ark is also called the Ark of the Testimony.

What then is the testimony of God? In a simple word, the Ten Commandments are the testimony of God. We may have an inaccurate concept of the Ten Commandments, thinking that the Ten Commandments are not good because they always put demands on us and that since today we are no longer under the law, we can put the law aside. This kind of concept is not completely accurate. We need to see that the Ten Commandments are not only the laws of God and the demands of God but also the explanation and revelation of God. The laws and commandments declare to us God's nature, intention, procedures, and ways so that we may know what kind of God He is in the universe. Hence, we may say that the Ten Commandments are the embodiment of God. God could not have drawn a picture of Himself for the Israelites, because then they would have worshipped His picture throughout all the generations. Therefore, God used the Ten Commandments to explain Himself and testify of Himself. Hence, the Ten Commandments are the testimony of God. Furthermore, the Ten Commandments as the testimony of God were placed in the Ark, which was made of wood overlaid with gold, and this Ark was called the Ark of the Testimony.

The Ark of the Testimony in the tabernacle was a type of Christ. The gold signifies divinity, and the wood signifies humanity. Hence, the ark made of wood overlaid with gold typifies the Lord Jesus as the One with two natures—the divine nature and the human nature. He was God who became a man, and in Him were the human nature and the divine nature. Divinity and humanity were completely mingled in Him. Therefore, the Lord Jesus was the reality of the Ark of the Testimony. The spiritual meaning of the Ten Commandments being placed in the Ark of the Testimony is that the entire explanation of God is in Christ. Christ is the explanation and embodiment of the invisible God. If you want to know what God is like, you have to come to Christ to find out. This is exactly like the situation in the New Jerusalem. In the New Jerusalem, Christ is the lamp and God is the light, and God as the light shines through Christ as the lamp. Therefore, Christ is the testimony of God, and as such, He is the source of all our experiences in the Holy Place.

The Supply of the Showbread Table

Because Christ has become our life, we can experience Him as our bread of life. Therefore, we come to the showbread table, which is the second piece of furniture in the tabernacle. The fact that the showbread table was also made of wood overlaid with gold spiritually means that it comes out from the Ark of the Testimony. The Christ with two natures, divinity and humanity, is the heavenly bread given by God to us that we can live by Him in the presence of God.

The Shining of the Golden Lampstand

The third item of furniture in the tabernacle is the golden lampstand. Whenever we experience Christ as our food and our life supply, inwardly we become bright and shining. In the morning if you do not eat the Lord to the full and once again enjoy the Lord, then you will not only be empty but also dark within. Your condition will be like that of the earth in Genesis 1, which says that there was "waste and emptiness, and darkness was on the surface of the deep" (v. 2). However, in the morning if you properly enjoy the Lord as the bread of life by eating and drinking of Him to the full, and if you are satisfied in this way, then inwardly you will be bright. This is exactly the order of our experience. The satisfaction with the bread of life brings in the shining of the light of life. Therefore, the golden lampstand is a type of the incarnated Lord Jesus entering into us to be our light of life.

The Acceptance of the Golden Incense Altar

At this point, we need to realize that Christ is also our golden incense altar. In Christ we can offer fragrant prayers to God and be acceptable to God. I believe that all of us have had this kind of experience. Whenever we enjoy Him and are satisfied and enlightened within by enjoying Him as the bread of life and the light of life, then immediately we feel that we are in the presence of God and that between us and God there is a fragrant odor. We sense that we have been accepted before God, and therefore, we thank, praise, and worship Him.

BEING A CHRISTIAN HINGING ON
THE EXPERIENCE OF CHRIST AS LIFE

We have clearly seen that being a Christian is not only a matter of living a proper human life outwardly but even more a matter of living by the life of the pure gold within. Today

God in Christ dwells in us as our life, and our experiences as Christians altogether hinge on how we deal with this Christ. Christ is the One who is both God and man. He is the embodiment of God, and in Him all the fullness of the Godhead dwells bodily. When we draw near to Him and receive Him, He becomes our life supply and our satisfaction. When we are satisfied with Him, we have the brightness and sweetness within. At such a time the sense of sweetness between God and us and the fragrance in the presence of God are truly indescribable. Thus, the only thing we can do is to praise and worship. These experiences are indications that we have experienced the Ark, the showbread table, the golden lampstand, and the golden incense altar. Whoever touches these matters is an inward Christian. Such a one not only has the fine white linen hangings without but also the precious, pure gold within. Hallelujah, we have the life of the pure gold within us. We should have a set of experiences pertaining to the pure gold within us. Every morning in our morning watch we should touch the Ark overlaid with gold, the showbread table also overlaid with gold, the lampstand of pure gold, and the golden incense altar.

To reach this stage is truly quite rare and precious. With many brothers and sisters, the fine white linen hangings have not yet been set up, not to mention the fact that there is no pure gold within them! If you have the fine white linen hangings without and are full of the pure gold within, your situation is truly quite good. However, I would like you to see that it is not enough even to be at this stage, because at this stage there still is no tabernacle in which God can dwell.

THE BUILDING OF THE BOARDS

I have heard that among the brothers and sisters there seems to be a kind of talk in which some are saying, "What difference does it make whether or not we have the building? It is all right as long as we have Christ." In other words, they are saying that it is enough merely to have the pure gold, so why do we need to talk about building? To such brothers and sisters I would like to ask whether or not it was enough that in Genesis 2 there was gold, pearl, and precious stone. If it were enough, then why is it that the will of God is not accomplished until the end of Revelation, when God has built the gold, pearl, and precious stone into a city as His tabernacle? May God have mercy upon us, and may He open our eyes to see that there is the need for building after receiving the pure gold. Only after the building takes place will there be the tabernacle, the dwelling place of God.

The Tabernacle Being the Enlargement of the Ark

Now let us briefly look at the tabernacle itself. The main components of the tabernacle were the standing boards. There were twenty on the south side, twenty on the north, and eight on the west, and all of them were made of wood overlaid with gold. What does this mean? Spiritually, this means that the tabernacle is the enlargement of the Ark. Just as the Ark was made of wood overlaid with gold, so the tabernacle was also constructed with wood overlaid with gold. The Ark enlarged is the tabernacle. The meaning of this is very deep. This means that the church is nothing other than the enlargement of Christ. Christ is God mingled with man, and the church is the enlargement of God's being mingled with man. Please remember that you are a board and that in you there is the life of God and the mingling of divinity and humanity. I am also a board, and in me there is also the mingling of divinity and humanity. Every saved person is a board, and when all the saved ones are connected and coordinated together, they become the tabernacle. It is a marvelous matter that the Bible has no record of how many pieces of wood were used to build the Ark. It seems that the Ark was made of a single, solid piece of wood. The tabernacle, however, was constructed with forty-eight standing boards. This indicates that the church is composed of many saved ones.

The Meaning of One and a Half Cubits

The boards were ten cubits in length and one and a half cubits in width. These measurements are also very meaningful. In many instances, the basic numbers of God's building were the numbers three and five or multiples of these numbers. One example is the altar, which was square—five cubits wide by five cubits long and three cubits high. Another example is the ark, which was two and a half cubits in length and one and a half cubits in width and in height. These measurements are one-half of the numbers five and three respectively. The width of each board was one and a half cubits, which is also one-half of the number three. This implies that only when two boards are put together to form three cubits can there be the number of building. What this means is that every brother or sister is only one and a half cubits and that each one needs another one to match him to become a whole unit. This corresponds with the principle in the New Testament. Recall that when the Lord Jesus sent out the disciples, He sent them two by two. Therefore, Peter was one and a half cubits, and John was also one and a half cubits. They served God together and could not be separated or divided. This is called coordination, and this is the building. The problem is that some brothers and sisters think that they are three cubits by themselves and do not need others to match them. Such brothers and sisters think that they can be Christians alone and do not need others at all.

Please remember that you will always be only one and a half cubits, half of a unit. You are only a member, not the whole body. Therefore, you need others to coordinate with you. Even if you are as great as the apostle Paul, you are still just a member and not the whole Body. Therefore, not one Christian can be independent. If it were possible to be independent Christians, then there would be no need for the church. Let me tell you before God that if I were to be separated from my brothers and sisters, I would have no way to be a Christian, and even more, I would have no way to serve God. Maybe some of you would say, "Have you not been ministering the word to us all this time? You must be very strong." However, I would like to tell you that no matter how strong I am, I am only one and a half cubits. Therefore, I cannot be independent. Rather, I need to coordinate with others.

When I was first saved, I could read the Bible by myself, I could pray alone, and I could pursue the Lord with great vigor on my own. Today, however, I feel more and more as if I cannot pray by myself anymore and that I have to find another brother to pray with me. When I was young, my strength to push ahead was very great. I was not afraid of anything, and I went everywhere to preach the gospel. Now wherever I go to preach the gospel, I always need a brother to go with me. This is because I know that since I am only one and a half cubits, I need a brother to coordinate with me so that I can stand firmly and be a whole unit.

On the day of Pentecost when Peter stood up to speak, the Bible says, "Peter, standing with the eleven, lifted up his voice and spoke forth" (Acts 2:14a). This is the principle of coordination. We need to learn a serious lesson—that no matter how great our gift is and no matter how weighty we are spiritually, we are still only one and a half cubits.

There is a certain matter recorded in the Bible which I feel is very sweet. When Paul wrote his first Epistle to the Corinthians, he began by saying, "Paul, a called apostle of Christ Jesus...and Sosthenes the brother, to the church of God which is in Corinth" (1:1-2). Paul did not write to the church in Corinth by himself alone as one and a half cubits. Rather, he sought another brother who was also one and a half cubits to coordinate with him. Paul realized the preciousness of the brothers. In those days the apostles did not act individualistically but in coordination. How I wish that we all knew how much we need the supply and coordination of the members. When we have this kind of feeling, then we can be built with others and can also build others.

Two Tenons with Two Corresponding Sockets

Not only so, underneath each board were two tenons that were inserted into two sockets of silver. In other words, there were two tenons with two corresponding sockets. Our concept is that it would be more convenient to have one tenon set against one socket, but God's thought is not like this. This is also a matter of building. If there was only one tenon, there would be no need for confirmation. Some brothers and sisters change so easily. The day before yesterday their condition was excellent, and yesterday it was also good, but today their condition is very poor. The reason for their being easily changeable is their lack of confirmation. Such people, in whatever they do, always decide and act on their own. Furthermore, they often use spiritual expressions such as, "This is my inner feeling," or, "This is something of God," and therefore, there is no need for others' confirmation. We must realize that this is very dangerous.

The fact that each board was one and a half cubits in width indicates that we need to be connected with others. The fact that each board had two tenons fixed in two corresponding sockets indicates that we need others' confirmation. If in our living and work we constantly have the confirmation of the brothers and sisters, then we will surely be well-protected. Suppose one day a newly saved brother has a feeling to go see a movie. If he would go and fellowship with another brother to seek confirmation regarding his feeling, then he would surely be clear concerning God's will in this matter. Then he would have not only one tenon but two tenons in two corresponding sockets. In this way, he would be preserved. Although this is a very shallow example, it illustrates this most fundamental principle.

The Golden Rings and the Golden Bars

Lastly, on the boards overlaid with gold were rings of gold, and through these rings were bars overlaid with gold. Everything was golden. This means that you and I have to live in God, in Christ, and in the Holy Spirit. Only when we live in gold, are overlaid with gold, and are joined and united in gold can we all be one. If the gold covering had been removed from the forty-eight boards, then there would have been merely forty-eight individual boards, completely scattered. However, since they had been overlaid with gold and joined together in gold and through gold, they became a solid entity, a builded structure.

I say again that your measurement is one and a half cubits and that you are only half a unit, because you are a member and not the whole Body. You also need to have two tenons. If at present you have only one, you must go and find another. You definitely need two tenons for you to be stabilized and so that you would not waver. At the same time, you must realize that the coordination and oneness of the church, the church's being built, and the church's being one are altogether in the pure gold, that is, in God. When you live in God, I live in God, and all of us live in God, then we can be one.

I look to God to grant every brother and sister to see that we have to be built together with others so that God can have a dwelling place and that the way to be built is to know that each of us is only one and a half cubits, that each of us needs two tenons, and that each of us needs to be overlaid with gold and united through and in gold.

CHAPTER FIVE

THE BUILDING OF THE TEMPLE

Scripture Reading: 2 Chron. 1:4-7, 13, 15; 3:4-5, 15; 1 Chron. 22:4; 28:6; 29:1-9; 1 Kings 6:1-3, 7, 9, 21-22, 30-34; 2 Chron. 3:1, 6-7; 5:2-7

THE TABERNACLE BEING
THE ENLARGEMENT OF THE ARK

We have briefly seen the spiritual meaning of the tabernacle in the Old Testament in regard to the matter of building. God placed the Ten Commandments inside the Ark. The Ark typifies Christ, and the Ten Commandments are the embodiment of God. Thus, the Ten Commandments being inside the Ark typifies God being expressed in Christ bodily. Furthermore, the Ark being placed in the tabernacle typifies Christ being in the church. This situation is exactly the same as the situation in the New Jerusalem. In the New Jerusalem God is the light, the Lamb is the lamp, and the lamp is in the holy city New Jerusalem. This is the fulfillment of the word at the end of Ephesians 3, which says, "[To God] be the glory in the church and in Christ Jesus" (v. 21). Therefore, in the first step God had Christ as His vessel so that He could put Himself into Christ. Now in the second step He is gaining the church to be a vessel for His Son, Christ, that Christ may put Himself into the church. This is typified by the Ten Commandments being put into the Ark and the Ark being placed in the tabernacle.

We have also said that the tabernacle was the enlargement of the Ark. The Ark was made of acacia wood overlaid with gold, and the main part of the tabernacle was also made of acacia wood overlaid with gold. Therefore, in its spiritual significance, the tabernacle was the enlargement of the Ark. The Ark was the smaller vessel, and the tabernacle was the enlarged vessel. The components of both were wood overlaid with gold. However, the Ark and the tabernacle were different in two respects. First, the tabernacle was composed of forty-eight boards of wood, but the Ark was one, whole, solid entity. This depicts the truth that while the church is composed of many saints who have been coordinated together, Christ is uniquely one and is a complete whole. Second, each of the forty-eight boards had two silver sockets, whereas there was no element of silver with the Ark because Christ does not need to be redeemed. The saints in the church are not only of two natures—the divine nature and the human nature—but are also joined as one in the redemption of Christ to be the habitation of God.

I believe that at this point you should be very clear that God needs Christ to be His vessel and that Christ needs the church to be His enlarged vessel. We have to see these two levels or spiritual steps. The first step is the experience of the outer court. In the outer court were the bronze altar, the bronze laver for washing, and the hangings of fine white linen. This signifies that the newly saved ones should put in order and cleanse their outward living and walk. The second step is the experience signified by the showbread table, the golden lampstand, and the golden incense altar in the Holy Place and the Ark in the Holy of Holies. This step is much more advanced than the first step. It is at this juncture that we see that a Christian must not only care for his outward living and walk but also for the divine life within. Furthermore, we see that Christ is the embodiment of God, the expression of God bodily. He is the One with two natures—the divine nature and the human nature. Therefore, we enjoy Him as our life supply and enlightenment within to be accepted by God. All of these experiences are inward and should be the desire and pursuit of the children of God.

However, this step is not the final step. The final step is the producing of the tabernacle through the enlargement of the Ark. This indicates that our experience of the Christ within us issues in Christ being enlarged in us. Then we are united with all the saints in the life of Christ and are built into an enlarged vessel of God to be a dwelling place, a resting place, for God.

THE ISSUE OF THE BUILDING OF THE TABERNACLE

God's Glory Being Manifested

Immediately after the tabernacle of God was completed and raised up, two things happened. The first thing that happened was that the glory of God filled the tabernacle (Exo. 40:34-38). That was perhaps the first time in history that God's glory was physically manifested. What is God's glory? God's glory is simply God expressed. In the same way, the shining from an electric light bulb is the manifestation of electricity. It is electricity glorified.

The day the glory of God filled the tabernacle was truly a great moment, because God had gained a dwelling place on the earth. Suppose that there was a group of God's children who were truly willing to learn to mutually coordinate in the life of God and to be joined with one another and built together to be the Body as God's spiritual habitation so that God could rest in it. We would have to believe that wherever there was such a group of people, God Himself would be expressed and glorified among them! There is nothing on the earth that could be more glorious than this!

God's Word Being Revealed

The second thing that happened was that the word of God was revealed in the tabernacle. Before the tabernacle was raised up, God had spoken with Moses on Mount Sinai. We may recall that the situation manifested there was terrifying. However, after the tabernacle was raised up, the glory of God filled the tabernacle, and from then on, God spoke to Moses in the tabernacle (Lev. 1:1). In the New Testament it is recorded in the book of Acts that when the church of God was produced on the earth, the glory of God filled the church, and God spoke in the church, just as He did in the tabernacle in the Old Testament.

Do you want to see the glory of God? If you do, then you

must come to the builded church. Do you want to hear God's word? If you do, then you must again come to the builded church. The glory of God and the word of God are two great matters. The glory of God is the expression of God, and the word of God is the explanation of God. God can be expressed only in the builded church, and God's word can be revealed only in the builded church.

THE TABERNACLE BEING
THE CENTER OF THE LIFE OF GOD'S PEOPLE

From the time that the tabernacle was built, the children of Israel had the tabernacle as their center. They encamped with the tabernacle as their center, they moved with the tabernacle as their center, they worshipped with the tabernacle as their center, and they fought with the tabernacle as their center. Everything in the lives of the children of Israel was centered on the tabernacle, and the tabernacle was centered on the Ark. Today it is the same with the church on the earth. Whether in relation to our work, service, worship, or warfare, we as the children of God should have the church as our center, and the church must have Christ as its center. Within the tabernacle there had to be the Ark, and outside of the Ark there had to be the tabernacle. Today it is the same. If we want to have Christ, we must have the church, and if we want to have the church, we must have Christ. Christ is the content of the church, and the church is the expression of Christ. The mutual matching of these two constitutes a normal situation.

THE SEPARATION OF THE ARK FROM THE TABERNACLE
AND THE RECOVERY OF THE ARK

It is a pity that this situation was maintained for only a short time before the Israelites became degraded and fell into desolation. As recorded in the book of 1 Samuel, the people of Israel fought with their enemy and were defeated, and the Ark of God was captured. The Ark was taken into the land of the Philistines and brought into the temple of their idol. However, God protected the Ark by His divine power, and as a result, the Philistines returned the Ark, sending it into the midst of the people of God. The Israelites, however, did not return the Ark to the tabernacle. Instead, they brought the Ark to the house of Abinadab and, subsequently, into the house of Obed-edom. At that time the Ark was separated from the tabernacle. That was a very abnormal situation. If you read church history, you will see that the same kind of situation occurred in the church. Whenever the church was in desolation and was abnormal, it seemed that Christ had been captured. In other words, it seemed that Christ had departed from the church and was separated from the church. Today you cannot find Christ in the formal churches. Rather, you see Christ mainly in the homes of the individual believers and in the individual believers themselves. This, however, is not the normal condition of the church.

This condition of the Ark being separated from the tabernacle continued until David came and there was a new recovery. As a man according to God's heart, David had a desire to build a temple for God so that God might have a resting place on the earth. Therefore, he brought the Ark of God into the city of David, which was on Mount Zion at the center of Jerusalem, and set the Ark in the tent which he had pitched especially for God.

In principle, what David did was right, because the Ark could not be without a tent. However, in a finer sense, this brought in a very delicate problem, because at that time there were two tents. The first one was the original tent, which first had been kept in Shiloh and then later had been moved to Gibeon. The other tent was the tent that David had pitched in his own city. The former tent had been built by Moses according to the pattern that God had revealed to him on the mountain, but during David's time it had lost the Ark and was separated from the Ark. The latter tent pitched by David had been pitched not through the revelation of God or according to the pattern shown on the mountain but according to David's good heart and intention, yet within it was the Ark. This was a very delicate matter. In church history there have been many similar situations. Sometimes when the church was in desolation, Christ and the church were completely separated, and all that was left of the so-called church was a formal facade. Instead, the presence of Christ could be touched in the homes of the saints who loved the Lord with a pure heart. Like David, these saints had the heart to prepare the church for Christ, yet their preparation was not according to the original revelation and pattern. No doubt, in principle, this kind of desire was good, but what they did could not last to eternity because it was not out of God and was not what God wanted.

Later, David wanted to build a house for God, and this desire was pleasing to God. However, because he was a man of war, and there was still no peace in the land, God did not let him accomplish this matter. For the rest of his life, David then prepared all the materials for the temple of God.

When Solomon succeeded his father, David, to the throne, the first thing he did after he became king was to go to the tabernacle at Gibeon, and there he worshipped and offered sacrifices to God. Solomon led his servants and the people there, and he offered one thousand burnt offerings. At Gibeon during the night, God visited Solomon and appeared to him in a dream, asking him what he desired to have. Solomon did not ask for anything for himself but only asked God to give him wisdom. God granted him his request and gave him wisdom. After Solomon awoke from his dream, he immediately left Gibeon and went back to Jerusalem. There he stood before the Ark of God and offered burnt offerings and peace offerings. This shows us that after Solomon received the wisdom of God, he realized that the tabernacle without the Ark was empty and that it had only an appearance and not much value. This implies that regardless of how proper a church is in appearance, as long as it does not have Christ as its content, then in the sight of God it is empty, having only an appearance but not much spiritual worth. Once Solomon received God's revelation and wisdom, he immediately left the empty tabernacle at Gibeon and returned to the Ark of God at Jerusalem. However, Solomon was not satisfied with the Ark alone, for he knew that although the tabernacle without the Ark was an empty shell, the Ark without the tabernacle was also something abnormal. Therefore, not long afterward, Solomon began to build a permanent tent, the temple, for the Ark.

If a church looks proper from the outside and is according to the pattern revealed by God on the mountain, but on the inside the Ark is nowhere to be found, that is, Christ cannot be contacted within it, then that church is merely an empty tabernacle and is worthless. On the other hand, to merely have the Ark does not mean that there are no problems. When the Ark was in the house of Obed-edom and when it was placed in the tent that David had pitched, it was still sojourning, staying in those places temporarily. Until the Ark found a proper tent or a fixed temple, it did not have a resting place (cf. Psa. 132). Therefore, we need to see that it was improper for the tabernacle to be without the Ark and that it was also abnormal for the Ark to be without the tabernacle. In other words, to have the church without Christ is improper, and to have Christ without the church is also abnormal. In a normal situation, it is necessary to have not only the Ark but also the tabernacle or the temple, which was a more permanent and enlarged tabernacle.

THE TEMPLE BEING
THE ENLARGED TABERNACLE

Now let us look at the story of the temple. The light of the truths in the Scriptures always shines brighter and brighter as one proceeds through the Scriptures. It is the same with the matter of building. Beginning with Abraham's life of pitching tents and building altars, the Bible reveals that God's desire is for His people to build a place on the earth for them to worship Him. However, Abraham's tents and altars were only a miniature of the building of God's dwelling place. They were like a small seed that had been sown into the ground and had not yet sprouted or budded. Later, Abraham's descendants multiplied, increased, and became the assembly of Israel. After they left Egypt and came to Mount Sinai, God revealed to them the pattern on the mountain through Moses. He wanted them to build a tabernacle and a bronze altar as well. This tabernacle and altar were much more concrete than the tents and altars that Abraham had built. Then when Solomon built the temple, the temple that he built was not only more concrete but also larger than the tabernacle raised up at the foot of Mount Sinai.

The tabernacle was ten cubits wide and thirty cubits long, and the temple was twenty cubits wide and sixty cubits long. Thus, the horizontal dimensions of the tabernacle were doubled in the temple. Furthermore, the tabernacle was ten cubits high, and the temple was thirty cubits high—three times higher than the tabernacle. Therefore, the temple was much larger than the tabernacle. Not only so, the temple was also more firmly fixed than the tabernacle. The tabernacle was movable. It was raised up by connecting the boards together, and it could be dismantled and moved at any time. Furthermore, when you looked upward from within the four sides of the tabernacle, what you saw was beautiful, but downward it was not good to look at. When you looked upward from within the tabernacle, everything that you saw was golden and very beautiful. However, if you looked down at the ground, what you saw was dirt because there was no flooring in the tabernacle. With the temple, however, the situation was different. The temple had huge precious stones as its foundation, so it was very stable, and its floor was made of cypress wood overlaid with gold, so it was also very firm.

This implies that as time goes on, the church will become larger and more stable. This has been the principle throughout the generations of church history. If we look back at the past thirty or forty years, we will see that the way that God took among us was also like this. Thirty years ago, our knowledge of the church somewhat had the flavor of Abraham's life of pitching tents and building altars. Gradually, the light concerning the church strengthened among us, and our situation became like the situation when the Israelites came to the foot of Mount Sinai and built the tabernacle. In the last three or five years, I deeply feel that among us there has been a little taste of a situation similar to the one when Solomon built the temple.

GOLD OVERLAYING THE WOOD
AND OIL BEING POURED UPON THE STONE

We need to mention another point concerning the temple.

Just as the Ark and the major parts inside the tabernacle were made of wood overlaid with gold, so it was with the interior of the temple. Wood overlaid with gold signifies the two natures—the human nature and the divine nature. I love these two phrases—*oil poured upon the stone* and *wood overlaid with gold*. The phrase *oil poured upon the stone* is the story of Bethel, and the phrase *wood overlaid with gold* is the story of the tabernacle and the temple. Both phrases speak of God coming to man to be mingled and joined with man as one. God's coming to the church, on the one hand, is a story of the oil being poured upon the stone. The Holy Spirit's descending on Peter and the rest of the believers on the day of Pentecost was truly a matter of the oil being poured upon the stone, resulting in the manifestation of Bethel, the house of God. On the other hand, God's coming to the church is also a story of wood being overlaid with gold. Peter and his companions were like pieces of strong acacia wood, and when the Spirit of God came upon them, they became like wood overlaid with gold. Humanly speaking, they were still acacia wood, but what was expressed through them was glowing gold. They were full of the element of God.

Three Kinds of Wood

We have to see that Christ is altogether a matter of mingling as symbolized by the Ark. The tabernacle and the temple were the enlargement of the Ark and were in the same principle, that is, the principle of the mingling of divinity with humanity. The temple, however, was quite particular in its constituents. For example, three kinds of wood were used in the temple: cypress, cedar, and olive wood.

Cypress

Let us first look at cypress. Like the Chinese, the ancient Jewish people had the custom of planting cypress trees in the ground above their graves. Therefore, in its spiritual significance, the cypress tree signifies death, and in particular, the death of Christ and the death of those who have died with Christ. The doors of the temple were made of cypress wood, signifying that the death of the Lord Jesus is the great entrance into the church.

Cedar

Next is cedar wood. This kind of wood, which came from Lebanon, grew on the high mountains. Today the national emblem on the flag of Lebanon is the cedar tree, which grows abundantly in that country. From a spiritual perspective, cedar wood signifies the resurrected Christ and those who have been resurrected in Christ. In the temple everything from the ground up was constructed with cedar wood. This shows us that the church is being built upward in the resurrection of Christ.

Olive Wood

The third kind of wood is olive wood. Olive wood was used for the doors on which were carvings of cherubim. Olive oil typifies the Holy Spirit. Hence, olive wood signifies the Christ in the Holy Spirit and those who are filled with the Holy Spirit. The doors of olive wood with the carvings of cherubim signify the Holy Spirit as the entrance to spiritual matters.

In summary, these three kinds of wood show us three great matters concerning the Lord Jesus. The first matter is that He died, the second matter is that He resurrected, and the third matter is that He became the Spirit. These three kinds of wood also show us who are the saved ones three aspects of our spiritual experience—our death with Christ, our resurrection with Christ, and our receiving the Holy Spirit with Christ. All those who want to be built together in the church must first be those who have died with Christ; that is, they must be cypress. Second, they must be those who have resurrected with Christ; that is, they must be cedar. Third, they must be those who are in the Holy Spirit with Christ, who have gained a spiritual entrance into spiritual matters and have a spiritual understanding of them, and upon whom the glory of God is manifest; that is, they must be olive wood. The church is constituted and built with these ones as materials. In the church there are no thorns, thistles, or other kinds of wood except cypress, cedar, and olive wood.

In other words, in the church there is only the new man in resurrection and in the Holy Spirit, and in this new man there cannot be Greek and Jew, circumcision and uncircumcision, barbarian, Scythian, slave, or free man, because all these have died and been buried with Christ.

Precious Stones

In the temple there were not only different kinds of wood but also stones, precious stones, and other materials. Hence, the temple was more particular than the tabernacle. We must not only be those who have died with Christ, who have resurrected with Christ, and who are in the Holy Spirit with Christ, but we must also be those who are transformed. Previously, we were earthen and made of clay. Romans 9 says that we are like lumps of clay in the hands of a potter, who out of the same lump makes some vessels unto honor and others unto dishonor. On the day we were saved, Christ added the element of God into us, and we were changed from clay into stones. Therefore, when Peter confessed to Jesus, "You are the Christ, the Son of the living God," the Lord told him right away, "Simon Barjona...you are Peter" (Matt. 16:16-18). The name *Peter* means "a stone." Later on in his first Epistle, Peter tells us that we, the saved ones, coming to the Lord, are living stones being built up together (2:4-5). When we were saved and regenerated, we were definitely changed. We are no longer pieces of clay but have become stones. Nevertheless, we cannot remain in this state and be satisfied with ourselves. We still need to let the Holy Spirit continue to do the work of burning and pressing that we may be continually transformed until we become precious stones.

In the temple we cannot see any element of clay. Rather, all we can see is bronze, gold, and precious materials. Therefore, do not consider the building of the church to be an easy and simple matter. It is not a matter that can be accomplished in a day or two. Instead, it will take a long time and cannot be done hastily or impatiently. The temple was quite great. The Bible tells us that it took seven years and six months and the labor of over ten thousand men to complete the building of the entire temple. The project of building the temple was not carried out in a loose or careless way.

THE RENEWING AND ENLARGEMENT
OF THE FURNITURE OF THE TEMPLE

Finally, we also must see that not only was the temple larger, more stable, and more weighty than the tabernacle, but the furniture in the temple was also made anew, and their dimensions were increased. The altar, the laver, the showbread table, the golden lampstand, and the incense altar were all reconstructed, and in most cases their dimensions were increased. In the tabernacle the altar had been five cubits square and three cubits high, but in the temple it was twenty cubits square and ten cubits high. In the tabernacle there had been only one golden lampstand, but in the temple there were ten of them. In the tabernacle there had been only one showbread table and one laver, but in the temple there were ten showbread tables and ten lavers. Everything in the temple was renewed and enlarged.

The only item that remained unchanged, that was not replaced, and that did not increase in size was the Ark. We know that the Ark was a type of Christ Himself. Our Lord is the same yesterday, today, and forever. He is the Lord who is ever new, so He does not need to be renewed. Moreover, He is eternally complete and perfect, so He does not need to be made larger.

However, our experience of Christ should change. Our experience of the cross, the Holy Spirit, and Christ as our life, light, acceptance, and sweetness should be renewed, deepened, and enlarged. This is very much according to the principle of the temple. The enlargement of the temple signifies the strengthening of the church, and the renewing and enlargement of the furniture in the temple signifies the renewing and enlargement of the saints' experience of Christ.

This picture indicates that our spiritual experience must match the stature of the church. We cannot have a large church yet be lacking in spiritual experience. This would be like having a huge temple yet having small lampstands, small showbread tables, small altars, and small lavers. The temple and the furniture would be incompatible. Therefore, in a church of considerable size, the size of the altar (that is, the experience of the cross) must be proportionately increased. The preaching of the gospel must be with greater impact so that when people come in, they would be strongly convicted and saved. At the same time, the believers' consecration to God must also be increased so that there is truly a large altar. Furthermore, when the church is enlarged, there must be the enlargement of the bronze laver. In other words, the enlightenment of the Holy Spirit and the washing by the Holy Spirit must be more intense, frequent, and renewing. In the same way, the showbread table and the golden lampstand, which signify Christ as our life supply and light, must also be enlarged. In addition, the golden incense altar (that is, our fellowship with God and our experience of being accepted by Him in Christ) also must be strengthened, increased, and enlarged.

We must see that the temple was focused on the unchangeable Christ. In other words, Christ is the center of the church, and He is also the center of all of the saints' spiritual experiences. Christ is forever the same, but the church must gradually be strengthened and enlarged, and the saints' spiritual experiences must also gradually be renewed and enlarged. These two—Christ and the church—must match each other. Neither can be lacking. In this way, we will not have a mere outward, empty shell without the rich, inward content, nor will we have merely the content without the matching outward appearance. The normal building of the church can be manifested only when both the inside and the outside are complete. May God be gracious to us!

CHAPTER SIX

FOUR SITUATIONS OF THE TABERNACLE

Scripture Reading: 1 Chron. 28:11-19; 22:5-10; 2 Kings 25:8-10; Ezra 1:1-7; Hag. 1:2-11

After reading these messages, we should be able to clearly see that the problem in the universe today is not with Christ but with the church. In the type of the tabernacle, the problem was not with the Ark. Rather, all the problems were with the tabernacle.

FOUR SITUATIONS OF THE TABERNACLE

If we read through the records concerning the history of the tabernacle and the Ark in the Old Testament, we will see that the Ark was unchanging but that the tabernacle, which was related to the Ark, went through four different situations. In other words, the tabernacle, which was in coordination with the Ark, was always in one of four different situations. If we compare these four situations with the situations of the church in her two thousand-year history on the earth, we will see that the situations of the tabernacle correspond exactly with the situations of the church from its beginning to the present. Now let us briefly point out these four kinds of situations.

The First Situation—
the Tabernacle without the Ark in It

The first situation is the one in which the tabernacle did not have the Ark in it. This occurred at the time when Eli was a judge. The Ark was captured by the Philistines, and the tabernacle was left in Shiloh. Spiritually, this typifies the church when it is without Christ and has become an empty shell. In this situation the church is the church in name, but it does not have Christ as its reality. In other words, the church has only an outward form and does not have Christ as its inward reality. This is the condition of the church in serious degradation.

The Second Situation—
the Ark without the Tabernacle

The second situation, which is the reverse of the first, is the situation in which the Ark was without the tabernacle. The Ark eventually was sent to the house of Obed-edom, but the tabernacle remained at Shiloh. The two were completely separated. Spiritually, this typifies a situation in which Christ is present, but there is no church to match Him. Ever since the church began to have problems and was taken captive by Roman Catholicism, which is today's Babylon, there have been many believers who were quite godly and in whom one could definitely see the Ark, Christ, but not the tabernacle, the church.

The Third Situation—
the Ark without the Proper Tabernacle

The third situation is the one in which the Ark and the tabernacle were both present, but the condition of the tabernacle was improper. David was a man after God's heart, so one day, out of consideration for the Ark of God, David brought the Ark into the city of David, which was on Mount Zion, a high mountain in the city of Jerusalem. There he pitched a tent for the Ark. However, this tent was not the original tent. The original tent had been built by Moses according to the heavenly pattern that God had revealed to him on Mount Sinai. Only that tent was according to God's heart because it had been built according to God's measurements and was therefore what God wanted. David's intention and motive were right, but he pitched a tent for the Ark according to his own pattern. In the eyes of God, this tent was improper and was not what He desired in His heart.

In church history there have been similar situations. In the past, some Christians, because they realized that the presence of Christ was with them individually and were thereby blessed by God, set up meetings for themselves out of their good intentions. However, those meetings were not the proper church meetings, just as the tent in the city of David was improper because it had not been pitched according to the heavenly pattern. On the one hand, those Christians were in a good situation because they did not live as individual Christians but had a meeting in which they worshipped the Lord together. On the other hand, they were not in a proper situation as the church in the beginning had been.

Suppose Peter and all the other apostles are in Jerusalem. Should he establish only one church in this city according to God's desire, or should he establish more than one church? Suppose Peter establishes only one church according to God's desire, but later Paul comes. Peter grew up in Judea, was saved and trained in Judea, and had been working in Judea, while Paul grew up in the Gentile world, was saved and trained in the Gentile world, and had been working in the Gentile world. Hence, Peter and Paul often dispute concerning the truth. Feeling that he has no way to work with Peter in Jerusalem, Paul begins to preach the gospel by himself, and as a result, many people are saved. These saved ones follow Paul to establish another meeting apart from the church already established by Peter. The gospels that Peter and Paul preach are the same, and the spiritual messages that they give are also similarly accurate. Furthermore, they both pay attention to the spiritual content and experiences of the bronze altar, the bronze laver, the showbread table, the golden lampstand, the golden incense altar, and the Ark. They also preach spiritual messages concerning Christ, the cross, the Holy Spirit, and life. However, eventually a problem arises. The meeting established by Paul and the church established by Peter become completely divided. Is this situation right or wrong? This situation is wrong! In this situation we can see that although Paul was spiritual, had a good heart, and did a good deed, the meeting he established was altogether not according to the original pattern. In a similar way, David pitched another tent that God could not acknowledge in His heart.

What is the original pattern? According to the original pattern, there can be only one church in Jerusalem. There cannot be more than one church. The divisive meeting that Paul established might have had the "Ark," but the "tabernacle" would not have been right. The Christ and the cross that they preached may have been right, but their meetings would not have been right. This is the third kind of situation, a situation in which one has the Ark but not the proper tabernacle.

A few years ago I visited a friend in Taiwan who asked me a question, saying, "Brother Lee, why is it that your meeting is right but a smaller meeting in another place is not right?" I said, "This question is not easy to answer. I am afraid that the more I answer, the more misunderstanding there will be." He then said, "You preach the cross, and they also preach the cross! You expound the Bible, and they also expound the Bible! You help the believers to be spiritual, and they do the same, perhaps even more than you do!" I replied, "Thank and praise the Lord. That is very good." He went on, saying, "You pay attention to the outward filling of the Holy Spirit, and they also pay attention to this!" I said, "It is not necessarily good to pay too much attention to the outward filling of the Holy Spirit, because we have discovered that in some places where the believers pay too much attention to this matter, problems tend to arise." He said, "There is a small meeting in which the believers are absolutely for the outward filling of the Holy Spirit, and on this point they are stronger than you." I said, "Thank and praise the Lord!" Finally, he brought up the initial question again and asked, "Brother Lee, why is it that your meeting is right but others' meetings are not right?"

This question was very difficult to answer. I could only turn around and ask the brother in return, "In the early days, during the time of the apostles, was there one church in a city, or could there have been more than one church in a city?" He answered, "It did not matter. It was all right as long as the believers preached the gospel and brought people to salvation. It was all right as long as the believers pursued being outwardly filled with the Holy Spirit and paid attention to being spiritual." In terms of the type of the tabernacle, what he was actually saying was, "It is all right as long as we have the Ark. Who cares about the tabernacle? It does not matter whether or not we have the tabernacle!" I then said to him in all sincerity, "Brother, we cannot be so quick to say that the matter of the church does not matter. According to the Scriptures, this is a big matter. For instance, in the beginning in Jerusalem three thousand people were saved, and later five thousand were saved. They met separately in many, many homes, but they were still one church. Nowhere does it say that in Jerusalem there were two churches. However, why is it that today in Taipei there is a church on almost every street and sometimes even several churches on one street? Is this city not turning into a 'church market'? In the Scriptures, there is only one church in a city or locality, such as the church in Jerusalem, the church in Antioch, the church in Ephesus, the church in Rome, and the church in Smyrna. In the Bible there is no such thing as a 'street church.'"

These days I am discovering more and more that the building of the church is the most confusing and neglected matter to the children of God. They have no problems concerning the gospel, concerning being spiritual, or concerning Christ. However, most are not clear concerning the matter of the tabernacle, the matter of the church. During my last trip to Tokyo, Japan, I was walking on the street one day when by chance I saw a place with a hanging sign that read, "Non-church-ism." I said to myself, "This is something new! I have been a Christian for thirty or forty years but have never seen a phrase like *non-church-ism*. Although Christianity today is in a state of confusion, most Christians have not gone so far as to say that they do not want the church. However, here are some people who are advocating non-church-ism!" How confusing the children of God have made the matter of the church on the earth today! It is so confusing that some are even saying, "Forget it! We do not care for the church!" In other words, they are saying, "We do not want the tabernacle because we want to avoid quarrelling!"

The Fourth Situation—
the Ark with the Proper Tabernacle

The third situation is the condition of Christianity today. I would like to ask you all again whether or not it is all right to have only the Ark. It is not all right! David was a man after God's heart. He cared about the matter of God's dwelling place very much. In Psalm 132 David swore and vowed to God, saying, "I shall not go into the tent of my house; / I shall not go up onto the couch of my bed; / I shall not give sleep to my eyes, / Slumber to my eyelids; / Until I find a place for Jehovah, / A tabernacle for the Mighty One of Jacob" (vv. 3-5). He also prayed, "Arise, O Jehovah, unto Your resting place, / You and the Ark of Your strength" (v. 8). David knew that to have only the Ark was not sufficient and that there was the need for a dwelling place. So according to his good intention, he built a tent for God, knowing in his heart that this was only temporary and not permanent. Subsequently, he intended to build a house for God. Then, through the prophet Nathan, God told David that although his intention was right, the time was not right, because the enemies had not yet been completely subdued, and there was not yet rest all around. Therefore, God told him that a son would be born to him and that his son would be a man of rest, and it was he who would build a house for God. Not only so, God also revealed to David the pattern of the temple through His Spirit, just as He revealed to Moses the pattern of the tabernacle on the mountain. Before his death, David clearly showed Solomon this pattern. Later Solomon built the temple according to the pattern that his father had showed him. The temple was what God in His heart wanted to obtain and to dwell in. Only when the temple was finished did the Ark of God have a proper and fixed dwelling place. This is the fourth kind of situation. In this situation, there is not only Christ who is so rich but also the church that is proper, strengthened, enlarged, and stabilized.

I believe that now you can clearly see this matter of a proper church not only needing to have Christ within but also needing to be built according to the pattern on the mountain. I will give a detailed explanation of the pattern on the mountain later. First, I must give you all a principle—there can be only one church in a locality. Only by keeping this principle can the children of God be guarded from division. It is a pity that today very few people abide by this principle. Almost everyone does as he wishes and considers this a matter of no consequence.

I was twenty years old and was just beginning to pursue the Lord fervently when, after seeing this light from the Bible, I discussed this matter with an old pastor. The old pastor was a very godly man who lived in God's presence. He said to me, "Mr. Lee, what you have seen may be considered very correct, and this record is truly in the Bible. However, in my opinion, a city with many separate churches has an advantage." I was very surprised and asked him, "What is the advantage?" He replied, "A church is a lampstand. If a city has only one church, then no matter how big the church is, it cannot shine brightly enough to cover the entire city. However, thank and praise the Lord that God in His great wisdom has allowed His children to be divided. The more they are divided, the more churches there are. On the surface, the church is being divided, but because of this division, God can have many small lampstands in a city. Thus, will not the entire city be illuminated?" His explanation was very clever. However, is this a divine pattern or a human pattern? The problems that we encounter today are not concerning spiritual matters but concerning the matter of the church. In our speaking about the building of the church, we have seen that the problem is not with the Ark. Instead, the problem is entirely with the tabernacle. I believe that all of you have seen that God needs to gain a proper tabernacle on the earth to match the Ark. In other words, God needs to gain the proper church to match His glorious Son, Christ. We cannot pay attention merely to being spiritual and neglect the matching of the proper church.

THE BUILDING OF THE CHURCH
NEEDING TO BE BALANCED

We need to bring up still another point. In the record concerning Moses' building of the tabernacle, the Bible mentions the dimensions of the various furnishings, but it does not tell us their weights. However, when God revealed the pattern of the temple to David, David not only saw the dimensions of the various furnishings, but he was also given their weights, such as the weights of the golden lampstands, the golden show-bread tables, and the golden incense altar. The Bible gives a clear record of all these weights. In particular, there is a very good utterance in 1 Chronicles 28:15, which says, "By weight for each...according to the service of each kind...." In other words, the weight of each item was fitting for its service. The light in the Bible is progressive; it shines brighter and clearer as one proceeds through the Bible. The light concerning God's building is surely more complete and more advanced with the temple than it is with the tabernacle, because the record of the temple mentions not only the dimensions but also the weights of the furnishings. This indicates that the basic prin-ciple in the building of the church is that everything must be balanced. What does the Bible mean when it says that the weights of the furnishings are fitting? This indicates that nothing in the church is too heavy or too light. In other words, nothing weighs either more or less than the measure of its usefulness. Suppose Solomon had built ten very large show-bread tables and ten very small lampstands. If he had put all of them together in the temple, would they have been balanced? You would have had the sense that they were so unbalanced! God's desire is to make all the vessels in the church very balanced, with the proper sizes and the fitting weights.

Perhaps some of you are still unclear about the meaning of being balanced. Let me give you a few illustrations. Suppose a certain brother has gained a little experience of fellowship-ping with the Lord as signified by the golden incense altar in the temple. Because of this, he also helps others to pay atten-tion to the matter of fellowshipping with the Lord. It is not at all wrong for him to do this. However, suppose one day a problem arises, and then this brother begins to go around telling the saints that all spiritual experiences are worthless except for fellowshipping with the Lord, which is valuable. Of all the spiritual experiences, he especially magnifies the matter of fellowshipping with the Lord. If he sees a brother studying the Bible, underlining verses and taking notes, he tells him, "Oh, these are all dead letters. This kind of reading is all in the mind. Just read a few verses, and that is enough. It is better to pray more and to fellowship with the Lord more! Only fellowshipping with the Lord is precious!" If he sees a brother coming to listen to messages on the Lord's Day, Thursday, and Saturday, he admonishes him, saying, "You do not have to listen to so many messages. All that the messages can give you is knowledge, and we know that knowledge puffs up. It is better that you pray more and fellowship with the Lord more!" In this brother's eyes, nothing is more important than having fellowship with the Lord. It is as if a large golden incense altar which fills up the entire temple has been built! Do not think that that I am joking. I have met this kind of brother before.

Let me give you another example. Suppose a brother has learned some lessons concerning reading the Scriptures. Consequently, he feels that nothing is as important as studying the Bible. When he sees the saints cleaning the chairs in the meeting hall, he tells them, "Oh, do not waste your precious time cleaning the chairs. You will never get into the New Jerusalem by cleaning the chairs. All these things will be burned. It is better to stay home and spend more time reading the Bible!" Such a one no longer has a fitting weight and has become unbalanced, because he considers the matter of reading the Bible to be too great and too important.

In another example, suppose a brother has learned some lessons about obeying the inward feeling and the anointing. This is very good; there is nothing wrong with this. However, even this matter can be overly magnified. I have facts and evidence to prove that there are some believers who have learned to touch their inner feeling daily, yet they made many mistakes which gave rise to problems in the church.

We must properly learn to obey the inner feeling, but we absolutely must not magnify this matter too much. We must keep everything in balance. In the temple there should be the golden lampstands, the showbread tables, the golden incense altar, the bronze altar, the lavers, and especially the Ark. The weights of all these items should be proper and fitting. In the church we should help the saints to pay attention to the experience of fellowshipping with the Lord and at the same time

pay attention to spending time to study the Bible. Furthermore, we should help them not to neglect caring for the inner
feeling and to obey the teaching of the anointing. However, we
absolutely should not make any one of these matters too
great or too important. Otherwise, we will definitely cause
problems.

Some brothers and sisters are always lopsided when it
comes to spiritual matters. They lean either too far toward
one side or too far toward the other side. Therefore, we cannot
serve independently in the church because we need the other
members, our companions, to balance us. This is quite a difficult matter, because all human beings tend to be one-sided
and independent. We humans are the most troublesome
beings in the universe! Our Lord spent only six days to finish
creating the heavens and the earth. As the Scripture says,
"For He spoke, and it was; / He commanded, and it stood"
(Psa. 33:9). However, in His work to build the church, because
He has encountered troublesome people such as we, He still
has not been able to finish His building after two thousand
years.

Let me describe this matter by giving you a few more illustrations. For example, we always say that Christians should
not be independent but in coordination. However, sometimes
even our coordination may result in trouble. For instance, the
brothers and sisters who have learned the matter of fellowship may seek out and gather together those who have also
touched the matter of fellowship. Others who particularly
care for the inner feeling may meet together solely for touching the inner feeling. Still others who like outward activities
may go out together daily to distribute gospel tracts or stand
at the entrance of the meeting hall to serve as ushers. There
may be other brothers and sisters who are especially inter-
ested in studying the Bible, and they may come together daily
to study the Scriptures. As a result, those in the church with
the same interests come together and create small worlds for
themselves. This is truly a case of "birds of a feather flocking
together." Ultimately, alienation arises in the church, and in
more serious cases, the tragedy of division occurs.

We need to see that the weights of the various items in the

temple are all proper and fitting. We have to learn to put ourselves to death. Perhaps you like to quietly study the Bible. Although you may not be involved with the ushering service, you can speak with a brother who enjoys ushering. You can ask him how he is doing in his ushering and then ask him how he has been doing in his Bible reading in recent days. In this way the two of you can have some fellowship in a very spontaneous manner, each one having his own weight and not trampling on the other. In this manner the church will gradually be built up.

Our Lord likes to put those who have different dispositions together in coordination. The quiet ones are matched with the active ones, and the quick ones are paired with the slow ones. We can see this kind of arrangement by the Lord in many couples. It is difficult to find a husband and wife who are exactly alike. I believe that the Lord does this to balance us who are often one-sided. It is so in the family, and it is even more so in the church. The utterance in the Bible is, "By weight for each...according to the service of each kind...." The weights are proper and fitting. When we see any of the brothers or sisters in the church doing something for the Lord, as long as he or she is not sinning or going to the extreme, we must not express our dissent, no matter how disagreeable his or her actions are to our taste. We should say, "Hallelujah, thank and praise the Lord!" Remember that the need of the church is multifaceted. Every vessel, great or small, has an indispensable function. The difficulty in the church today is that when someone sees a certain spiritual matter, he then rises up to oppose others, and when another person sees a different spiritual matter, he rises up to oppose the first one.

I heard that in Southeast Asia there is a locality where the brothers use the messages given on the platform every Lord's Day to oppose each other. On one day one brother opposes another brother, and the next week the second brother opposes the first. For instance, on one Lord's Day a brother speaks about everything being by faith. Then the next Lord's Day another brother speaks about faith without works being dead. Then on the following Lord's Day the first speaker says that a work without faith is a dead work. Thus, one speaks about faith, and the other speaks about work. Both speak against each other on the platform. This kind of speaking is altogether done in a spirit of tearing down, a spirit of divisiveness, which frustrates the church from being built.

If you have been dealt with and have learned some lessons, then when someone talks about everything being by faith, you will let him speak this. After a period of time, when you have the opportunity, you may give a message as a supplement, saying that we should have faith but that in addition we should have the fruit or the work which is of faith. When you speak in this way, you do not have a spirit of contradiction. Instead, your message matches his message. One message complements the other. If someone is speaking heresy or is in serious error, then it is another matter. Otherwise, you should do your best to go along with others and to perfect others.

THE CHURCH BEING BUILT IN PEACE

Please remember that the temple was built in peace. The builder of the temple was Solomon, whose name means "peace." Whenever there is no peace in the church, there is no building. Today it is with a heavy heart that I say that this problem has been with the church for the past two thousand years. The building of the church requires gifts. Without gifts the church cannot be built. However, it is very troubling that once a church has gifts, the gifts often begin to fight with each other. If the gifts are relatively small, the fighting is not so serious, but if the gifts are bigger, the fighting is more intense. The building of the church requires a certain measure of spirituality. However, the problem is that whenever someone becomes somewhat spiritual, difficulties arise. One spiritual person will fight with another spiritual person, and as a result, both lose their spirituality. This is a situation in which the weights are not proper or fitting.

THE BUILDING OF THE CHURCH
BEING A MATTER FOR THE PRESENT DAY

Lastly, I would like to mention one more matter. David and

Solomon both occupied special positions in the building of the temple. The former prepared the building materials, and the latter accomplished the building. Most readers of the Bible acknowledge that David and Solomon both typify Christ. David's entire life was a type of Christ in His suffering, fighting, and crucifixion. Just as David in his sufferings prepared the building material for the temple, so also Christ in His sufferings and death redeemed and prepared us as the building material for the church. Solomon was a type of Christ in His resurrection, including His ascension and His coming back. Just as Solomon accomplished the building of the temple, Christ in His resurrection will build the church until His return.

Some say that the real building up of the church will not occur today but on the day of Christ's return. They say that today is the age of David, that is, the age of the church in suffering. At most it is the age in which the Lord is preparing the building material. This concept, however, is not accurate. Remember that the Lord Jesus said, "Destroy this temple, and in three days I will raise it up" (John 2:19). The Lord was speaking of the temple of His body (v. 21). In His resurrection His body became a mystical Body, the church. Hence, the building of the church is a matter in resurrection.

Not only so, if the building of the church were to be delayed until the Lord's return, then all of the records concerning the building of the church in Acts and in the Epistles would be empty words. The record of Acts clearly shows us that immediately after His death, resurrection, ascension, and descension in the Holy Spirit, the Lord began to build His church. He began from Jerusalem, spread to all of Judea, and then turned to the Gentiles. Eventually, He will reach the uttermost parts of the earth. Therefore, all that the Lord has been doing from the time of His resurrection and all that He will continue to do until the time of His return is to build up His church. Therefore, the building of the church has already begun today and does not have to be delayed until the future.

SATAN'S DESTRUCTION AND GOD'S RESTORATION

In the Old Testament we see that when the building of the

temple was completed, God's glory filled the temple. However, it is a pity that this situation did not last long. Not long afterward, the children of Israel failed and were ultimately taken captive to Babylon. Babylon was versus the building of God. God wants a building, but Satan also wants a building. The Bible tells us that the last city that Satan built was Babylon. One day the Babylonians came to Jerusalem, and they destroyed the temple as well as the city and even brought all the vessels that were in the temple for the worship of God (except the Ark, which was not mentioned) to Babylon and put them in the temple of their idol.

Why did the Bible not mention how God dealt with the Ark? The reason why the record of the Bible does not tell us this is to indicate that the church may be destroyed, but Christ cannot be destroyed. During the past two thousand years, the problem has never been with Christ but with the church. After the temple was built up, the Babylonian forces came and tried to tear it down. Many readers of the Bible acknowledge that Babylon typifies the organized Roman Catholic Church. This is Satan's stratagem to destroy the church.

Thank God that after seventy years, the time of the Israelites' captivity was fulfilled, and God moved King Cyrus and stirred up his spirit to let the Israelites return to Jerusalem for the rebuilding and recovery of the temple. The record of the Bible clearly shows us that while the enemy was trying to destroy the temple, God was focused on the recovery of the temple. None of the problems were with the Ark. Instead, all of the problems were with the tabernacle and with the temple. In other words, the problem is not with Christ but with the church. When we would read church history, we realize that beginning at Martin Luther's time, God's people began to come out from the Roman Catholic Church. Ever since that time, God's desire has been that we thoroughly come out of Babylon to recover the building of the church. We as a group of Christians are neither in the Roman Catholic Church nor in the Protestant churches. According to God's intention, we desire to be delivered out of every religious organization. According to the Old Testament type, our desire is to come out of Babylon and to return to the proper foundation and ground—which is the site of the former temple in Jerusalem, upon which our forefathers and the apostles worshipped God—to rebuild and recover the temple. We wish to return only to such a ground and foundation to meet, to worship God, and to establish the church.

I hope that all the children of God would see that the problem is not with the Ark but with the tabernacle and the temple. There is no problem with Christ. All the problems are with the church. Our Lord is eternally established and unchangeable. However, the dwelling place that He wants to obtain on the earth has been misunderstood by men as well as destroyed by the enemy. Therefore, like David, we should always consider God's heart's desire and regard as important what He regards as important. We must not only have the Ark, but we must also have the proper dwelling place. We must not only have Christ, but we must also have the proper church to match Christ. Only in this way can God's heart be fully satisfied, and only in this way can God be glorified in the church and in Christ. May the Lord bless us that we may treasure Him and likewise treasure His chosen and builded vessel, the church.

CHAPTER SEVEN

THE LIGHT ON
BUILDING IN THE NEW TESTAMENT

Scripture Reading: John 1:14; 2:19-22; Matt. 16:15-19; Acts 9:31; Eph. 2:20-22; Rev. 1:20; 21:14

THE CENTER OF THE NEW TESTAMENT ALSO BEING THE TABERNACLE AND THE TEMPLE

In this message we want to continue to see the vision concerning the building of the church in the New Testament. At the beginning we said that the Old Testament is focused on the tabernacle and the temple. Now we come to the New Testament, which is also centered on the tabernacle and the temple. The New Testament tells us that the Lord Jesus was the Word who became flesh and tabernacled among us (John 1:14). This turns us back to the story of the tabernacle in the Old Testament. In His coming to the earth the Lord Jesus was a tabernacle pitched among men.

Later, the disciples remembered that the Scriptures said that the Lord Jesus would be devoured by the zeal of God's house (2:17). Following this, He told them that His body was the temple of God. He said, "Destroy this temple, and in three days I will raise it up" (v. 19). What He meant was that one day the Jews would nail His body on the cross but that on the third day He would be resurrected. Afterward, this word of His was fulfilled. Furthermore, the Lord regenerated us who have believed into Him, and He imparted Himself into us as our life, thereby making us His mystical Body, the church. Both Paul and Peter tell us clearly in their Epistles that the church is the temple of God and the house built by God. Although the New Testament is composed of twenty-seven books, its center is still the tabernacle and the temple, which at the beginning denote Christ Himself but after Christ's death and resurrection denote the church as the enlargement of Christ.

In this message we will try to look briefly at the vision of the building of the church in the entire New Testament.

THE FOUR GOSPELS—
THE EMBODIMENT OF GOD IN CHRIST

The Bible truly is a marvelous book. If we read it with spiritual insight, the more we read it, the more we will discover that the Bible's line of thought is very meaningful. Now we want to consider the first four books of the New Testament—the Gospels—from the perspective of the types in the Old Testament. The four Gospels first speak about the Ten Commandments in the Ark, the Ten Commandments being the embodiment of God, and the Ark simply being Christ Himself. In other words, the central subject of the four Gospels is the embodiment of God in Christ. This is the story of Jesus the Nazarene.

We all know that the four Gospels begin by telling us that the Lord Jesus who came to be our Savior was called Emmanuel. The literal meaning of the name Emmanuel is "God with us." This does not merely refer to God being with us in an outward way by being among us. It also refers to God being with us by coming into us to be mingled with us. The end of the four Gospels shows us that this Emmanuel was transfigured after His death and resurrection into the Spirit so that He could enter into those who belong to Him and be united with them.

The Lord Jesus was truly Emmanuel. The record of the four Gospels, which concerns His living, speaking, action, and work, as well as all the miracles and wonders that He did, shows that He had two particular characteristics. On the one hand, His living was truly in the fashion of a man. One simply cannot deny that He was a man. He was the same as any ordinary man—He ate when He was hungry, He drank when He was thirsty, and He slept when He was tired. Moreover, He shed tears and wept when He was sorrowful. His countenance was no different from others, except that His visage and form were more marred than that of any man (Isa. 52:14). He was like a root out of dry ground and did not have an attracting form or beautiful appearance that people would desire Him (53:2). When people saw Him, they asked, "Is this not a man from Galilee? Is not this the carpenter's son?" He appeared to be a very common man among the people. On the other hand, however, His living, actions, and words often manifested something extraordinary. His words were simple, yet they contained the highest wisdom. For instance, He said, "I am the light of the world; he who follows Me shall by no means walk in darkness, but shall have the light of life" (John 8:12). This statement is very simple but very profound. In all of human history not one philosopher has dared to say such a thing before men. Furthermore, the Lord Jesus said, "If anyone thirsts, let him come to Me and drink. He who believes into Me, as the Scripture said, out of his innermost being shall flow rivers of living water" (7:37-38). This statement is also extremely great and wise. He also said, "I am the bread of life; he who comes to Me shall by no means hunger," and "Come to Me all who toil and are burdened, and I will give you rest" (6:35; Matt. 11:28). These words seem to be very simple, yet the meanings behind them are very rich. One must admit that the Lord Jesus was a most extraordinary man. No wonder a great philosopher once spoke of Him, saying that if the Lord Jesus recorded in the four Gospels had been fabricated by someone, then this fabricator would have been qualified to be the Lord Jesus! This is right.

The Lord Jesus was a very ordinary man on the one hand and a most unusual one on the other. No wonder those who followed Him often asked behind His back, "Who is this One?" On the one hand, He truly was a normal man, but on the other hand, He was quite extraordinary! Everyone who saw Him was perplexed, asking, "Who is He? Why is He so myste-rious?" He was mysterious because He was the God-man, Emmanuel.

One day when the Lord went into the region of Caesarea Philippi, He asked His disciples, "Who do men say that the

Son of Man is?" And they said, "Some, John the Baptist; and others, Elijah; and still others, Jeremiah or one of the prophets." He said to them, "But you, who do you say that I am?" And Simon Peter answered and said, "You are the Christ, the Son of the living God" (Matt. 16:13-16). This meant that the Lord was God expressed and the One who would accomplish the will of God in man. We can know God in this Nazarene. God expressed Himself bodily in this man. He was a hybrid, a mingling of God and man. This was typified by the Ten Commandments hidden in the Ark made of wood overlaid with gold, and this is what is recorded in the four Gospels.

THE ACTS—CHRIST ENLARGED TO BE THE CHURCH

However, is it enough merely to have the Ark? No, the Ark needs the tabernacle as its match. In other words, such a perfect Christ still needs the church as His match. Therefore, after the Gospels is the book of Acts, which shows us that after this God-man resurrected from among the dead, He was transfigured into the Holy Spirit and entered into everyone who believed into Him. This was the enlargement of the principle of incarnation, that is, the enlargement of the principle of wood overlaid with gold. The Ark was enlarged to be the tabernacle, and likewise Christ has been enlarged to be the church.

In the Gospels there was only an individual—Jesus the Nazarene. He alone was wood overlaid with gold. In Acts 1, however, there were at least one hundred and twenty Galileans, including Peter, James, and John, who were wood overlaid with gold. In a sense, they were the enlargement of Jesus the Nazarene in the Gospels. Furthermore, on the day of Pentecost three thousand persons were saved, and later five thousand more were added. All of them were also persons of wood overlaid with gold. They all had the life of Christ within them and had been baptized in the Holy Spirit into one Body, and like the standing boards that were united by the golden bars in the golden rings, they were being built together into a tabernacle, the church. Therefore, the tabernacle was the enlargement of the Ark, and the church is the enlargement of Christ. This is the enlargement of the principle of incarnation.

God was first expressed richly and bodily in Christ and is now expressed in the church.

A real Christian is one into whom Christ has entered. One time I asked someone who was a Christian, "Who are you?" Being puzzled by my question, he did not know how to answer. Then I asked again, "Please tell me, are you a man or are you Christ?" He said, "Of course, I am a man." Then I said, "Then are you Christ or not?" He said, "How could I say that I am Christ?" I said, "What is your relationship with Christ?" He answered, "I believe in Him as my Savior." I asked, "Is that all?" He answered, "That is about all." I asked, "Has Christ come into you?" He replied, "He has come in." I asked again, "Then what kind of man are you?" He answered, "I am just the kind of man that I am." How foolish was this person! Do not laugh at him, however, for we are often just as foolish. Eventually, I pointed to a glass of tea on the table and asked him, "What is in this glass?" He said, "It is tea, obviously!" I asked, "Is it not water?" He said, "The tea is in the water, so it is tea!" Then I asked him, "Since Christ is in you, who are you? Has there been a change in you?" Finally he understood and said, "Oh, I am Christ!"

Actually, what he said was not entirely accurate. The northern Chinese refer to tea as "tea-water." This is more accurate. When Christ came into us, we became Christ-men. When we are speaking of someone who is a Christian, what we are speaking of is not merely a disciple of Christ but a Christ-man, one who has Christ within. In Acts there was a group of Christ-men who were the enlargement of the Ark made of wood overlaid with gold. They had become the many standing boards made of wood overlaid with gold. This was the enlargement of the principle of incarnation, the mingling of two natures—divinity and humanity. These standing boards were united by the golden rings and golden bars and became the tabernacle, which is the church. This is what happened when the church was produced in the beginning at Pentecost. It began in Jerusalem, then it reached Samaria, and then it spread to all of Judea. At the present time, this expansion is still going on.

ROMANS—THE COMPONENTS OF THE CHURCH

In terms of typology, the four Gospels speak about the Ark, and Acts speaks about the tabernacle. Having the Ark itself is not enough. There is the need for the tabernacle as its match. However, the revelation of the Bible does not stop there. A thoughtful person would surely ask, "Now that we have the Ark and also the tabernacle, that is, Christ and the church, what kind of people are the components of the church?" If we say that they are the standing boards that are made of wood overlaid with gold, this person would surely continue to ask, "What kind of wood is it? How is it overlaid with gold?" The answer to these questions is in the Epistle to the Romans, the book immediately following Acts.

The book of Romans gives us a portrait of man. The beginning of Romans shows us that a person who does not know God and who rejects God commits all kinds of sins. Chapter two tells us that such a person, after being put under the law and living under his conscience, still commits sins. Chapter three shows us that this man, who is under God's condemnation, eventually is justified by believing in the Lord Jesus. In chapter four we see that this man is accepted by God through faith. Chapter five shows us that this man who was formerly in Adam is now in Christ. Chapter six tells us that through Christ's death this man has come out of Adam and through Christ's resurrection has been transferred into Christ. Chapter seven shows us that in the flesh this man can never please God. Chapter eight shows us that this man needs to live in the Holy Spirit and to walk according to the spirit that he may have life and peace, be pleasing to God, and eventually be conformed to the glorious image of God's Son. Chapters nine through eleven, which form a parenthetical section, speak concerning God's selection. Chapter twelve shows us that these ones who are living in the Holy Spirit and being conformed to the image of God's Son become components of the glorious church, which is a corporate man. These persons are like the standing boards of the tabernacle. They are the many members of the Body of Christ, joined together and coordinated with each other. Chapter thirteen to the end of the book speaks about the practical living of this Body in detail. Therefore, Romans explains to us what kind of people are the components of the church.

FIRST CORINTHIANS—
CHRIST AND THE CROSS NULLIFYING
THE FACTORS THAT DAMAGE THE CHURCH

Up to this point, everything has been quite clear. However, this matter is not so simple. Those who are the components of the church may still be under the control of the flesh and the influence of the world. Thus, it is still possible for problems to arise and for the building of the church to be damaged. Therefore, after Romans, 1 Corinthians shows us that there are two major factors that damage the church. One is the flesh within us, and the other is the world outside of us. For instance, concerning the problem of division in the church in Corinth, chapter one says, "Each of you says, I am of Paul, and I of Apollos, and I of Cephas, and I of Christ" (v. 12). Paul told them that the fact that they were divisive proved that they were fleshly and that they had been contaminated by the world and were walking according to the manner of man (3:3-4). Not only so, in the church in Corinth there were also the problems of fornication and of things sacrificed to idols. There was even a problem concerning spiritual gifts. Among them, some despised a particular gift, while others highly regarded that same gift. Both groups insisted on their own views. Please remember that these problems in the church in Corinth were typical. Some churches today have the same kinds of problems. Therefore, Paul in his Epistle asked the Corinthians, "Is Christ divided? Was Paul crucified for you?" (1:13). In 3:5-7 he said, "What then is Apollos? And what is Paul? Ministers through whom you believed, even as the Lord gave to each one of them. I planted, Apollos watered, but God caused the growth. So then neither is he who plants anything nor he who waters, but God who causes the growth." Moreover, he said, "So then let no one boast in men, for all things are yours, whether Paul or Apollos or Cephas or the world or life or death or things present or things to come; all are yours, but you are Christ's, and Christ is God's" (vv. 21-23). The gifts may be different, but they are all for the building up of the church of Christ. We must not because of the flesh appraise one gift higher than another, prefer one gift over another, or think more highly of our gift than others' gifts.

One day I gave a word of fellowship to the elders of the church in Taipei. I said that we should thank the Lord that today there is no one among us in whom the gift of healing has been especially manifested. Suppose that such a brother were raised up among us so that when he lays his hands on people and prays over them, their cancer is cured, their high blood pressure is lowered, the blind see, and the lame walk. If this happened, then all of us would have to give way to him and let him go everywhere to lay his hands on people to heal them! I believe that many brothers and sisters would follow him from Taipei to Hualien and then on to Tainan. Everyone would be amazed at this brother, and he himself would feel that he is something marvelous. The saints would be excited and unable to calm down. Eventually, the brothers and sisters would be unable to do anything else besides singing hallelujah, and we would have to give up any hope of building the church. In the end, a factor of division would be brought into the church. Then I asked the brothers what they would do if this kind of situation arose. Thank the Lord that in the first Epistle to the Corinthians, Paul not only pointed out the factors of division in the church on the negative side, but also spoke on the positive side concerning the way to nullify the factors of division. That way is Christ and His cross. As long as the church accepts the cross, the flesh will be dealt with. Then there will be no division in the church, and Christ will have the preeminence in the church.

One time a brother came to me and asked, "Brother Lee, a certain responsible brother in our home meeting said and did certain things. Do you think it is all right?" Then I turned the matter around and told him, "What that responsible brother said or did is secondary. Please calm down first and consider whether your speaking just now, including your intention, attitude, and tone, was in the Holy Spirit or in the flesh." He very honestly told me, "I know my speaking was in the flesh." Then I said, "Brother, as long as you are in the flesh, you have no ground to speak about anything. As long as we are in the flesh, we fall into the hand of Satan." He asked me again, "Then does this mean that I should not speak anything again?" I said, "I am not saying that you should not speak. What I am saying is that you should ask yourself where you are when you speak. Are you speaking in the flesh or in the Holy Spirit? If you are in the flesh, then you need to receive the cross of Christ. After you have received the cross, then you will know whether or not you should speak and to what extent you should speak." After a few days, this brother came back to tell me, "Brother Lee, thank the Lord that now I know how to speak!" Remember that Christ and the cross nullify the divisive factors within the brothers and sisters. This is what 1 Corinthians shows us.

SECOND CORINTHIANS—
THE MINISTERS FOR THE BUILDING OF THE CHURCH

Now we go on to 2 Corinthians. This book, which is deeper than 1 Corinthians, shows us that in the church there is a need for ministers who are for the building. Such ministers are persons who have practically experienced the breaking and tearing down by the cross and the full constituting work of the Holy Spirit. Paul was such a minister. First Corinthians says that when spiritual gifts fall into the possession of fleshly believers, such believers may become a trouble to the church. Spiritual gifts must be exercised by those who have passed through the breaking of the cross and who are full of the element of Christ within. Only then can they be a real benefit and help in building up the church. Otherwise, sooner or later they will produce a very great problem in the church. Therefore, 2 Corinthians deals with the matter of the ministry. Ministry is different from gift. A minister is not only a person with a spiritual gift but also a person who, in God's hand, has passed through burning, pressure, grinding, and breaking. Although his outer man is decaying, his inner man is being renewed day by day. Inwardly he is full of the life of Christ and the constitution of the Holy Spirit.

If a gifted person does not let Christ have the preeminence in him by passing through the dealing of the cross, then the gift in his hand will sooner or later become a problem to the church. Although his gift may seem to benefit the church somewhat in the beginning, in the end it will damage the building of the church. Strictly speaking, the real building up of the church depends not so much on the gifted persons but on ministers like Paul. Paul truly was one whom God had stripped, pressed, burned, beaten, ground, and broken numerous times. He was inwardly full of the constitution of the Holy Spirit and full of the element of life. His outer man was being consumed, but his inner man was being renewed day by day. He was not only a gifted person, but even more, he was a mature minister in God's hand. Only this kind of minister can cause the church to be truly built up. This is what 2 Corinthians particularly shows us.

GALATIANS—DELIVERANCE FROM
THE DISTURBANCE OF THE LAW

Now we go on to the book of Galatians. This book shows us that in the process of the building up of the church there is a serious and disturbing matter—the matter of the law and works. Those in the church who still try to live before God by depending on their works are a big problem to the building of the church. We must realize that all those who have been built into the church are living in Christ, having been freed from the law and from their own works. They have had Christ revealed in them, they have been crucified with Christ, they have been delivered from the control of the flesh through the cross of Christ, and they have been freed from the usurpation of the world so that it is no longer they who live, but it is Christ who lives in them. In everything they simply take Christ as their life until Christ is formed in them so that they become Christ-men in reality as well as in name. Only such ones can be built together to become the Body of Christ. This is what Galatians shows us.

EPHESIANS—
THE NATURE AND STATUSES OF THE CHURCH

After Galatians, Ephesians speaks even more clearly on the building of the church. In relation to Christ, the church is the Body of Christ, and in relation to God, the church is the dwelling place of God. Furthermore, in relation to the love of Christ, the church is the counterpart of Christ, in relation to God's warfare, the church is a warrior, and in relation to the nature of the church itself, the church is the new man. Therefore, chapter one says that the church is the Body, chapter two says that the church is the dwelling place, chapter four says that the church is the new man, chapter five says that the church is the wife, and chapter six says that the church is the warrior. These are the many expressions and statuses of the builded church.

PHILIPPIANS—THE LIVING OF THE CHURCH

Following Ephesians, Philippians shows us the practical living of those who are being built together in the church. Because these ones know the resurrected Christ and His resurrection power, they live in His resurrection life, and by His resurrection power they fellowship in His sufferings and die with Him, being conformed to His death.

COLOSSIANS—THE HEAD OF THE CHURCH

Following this, the book of Colossians tells us that when this kind of practical living is manifested in the church, then Christ immediately has the preeminence in everything in the believers in the church, and He fully manifests the authority and the riches of the Head. Then we are able to experience in the church all the riches in Christ.

FIRST AND SECOND THESSALONIANS— THE CHURCH AWAITING CHRIST'S RETURN FOR HER RAPTURE AND TRANSFIGURATION

At this point, we may say that there are no more problems with the church. She is nearly perfect. The only thing she needs to do is to wait for Christ's return, at which time she will be raptured, transfigured, and fully conformed to the glorious image of the Lord. This is recorded in 1 and 2 Thessalonians.

FIRST TIMOTHY, SECOND TIMOTHY, AND TITUS— THE PRACTICAL ASPECT OF THE CHURCH

Logically, the Bible could have ended with 2 Thessalonians. However, there is still another aspect of the church revealed in the Bible, and that aspect is the practice of the church. The church is the house of God, and a house involves many practical matters. For instance, how should the affairs of a church be administered locally? How should the church be taught? How should a church be led? How should one serve in a church? What are the qualifications for those who would administer and serve the church? These are all practical matters in the house of God. Therefore, the three books of 1 Timothy, 2 Timothy, and Titus are needed to deal particularly with the practice of the church. If the church is under the proper administration, then the church will become the pillar and base of the truth, that is, the mystery of godliness—God manifested in the flesh. Such a practical church is the house and resting place of the living God.

PHILEMON—THE LOVE IN THE CHURCH

After the three books of 1 and 2 Timothy and Titus is the book of Philemon, the shortest book in the Bible. I used to think, "Why was this book included in the Bible? What kind of position does it occupy in the Bible?" Then one day the Holy Spirit pointed out to me that the reason for including Philemon in the Bible was to show us that in the practical church, the relationship between two brothers must be based on a fundamental principle illustrated by the love of Philemon toward Onesimus. In the practical church the unique relationship among the saints is love, and this love is directed not only toward the lovable ones but also toward the unlovable ones. It is a matter of loving not only those who are your equal but also those who are not on an equal standing with you. Philemon was a master, and Onesimus was a slave, even a runaway slave. One day Onesimus was saved in a prison through Paul, and when he was released, Paul wrote this letter for him to bring to Philemon. In his letter Paul asked Philemon to receive Onesimus in love and to treat him as a brother. If today's church lacks this kind of love, then there will be a great problem when we talk about the practical church. Moreover, there will be no hope for the church in Philadelphia to be built up today.

Up to this point the New Testament has spoken very thoroughly concerning the building of the church, both in its spiritual aspect and in its practical aspect. However, there are still five more books in the New Testament: the Epistle to the Hebrews, the Epistle of James, the two Epistles of Peter, the three Epistles of John, and the Epistle of Jude. These five books may be considered as supplementary books.

HEBREWS—SOLVING THE PROBLEM OF JUDAISM

The book of Hebrews shows us how to solve the problem of the Jewish religion. Since Christ has already nullified Judaism, those who are in the church of Christ must not remain in the Jewish religion.

JAMES—WORKS AS A BALANCE TO FAITH

The book of James shows us how to balance empty faith with genuine works. If we talk about faith but do not have works, then that kind of faith is dead. Real faith produces the fruit of works.

FIRST AND SECOND PETER— GOD'S GOVERNMENTAL ADMINISTRATION

First and Second Peter speak about God's discipline and dealing in the church, or in other words, God's governmental administration. God not only rules over the unbelievers but even more governs His children. The children of God must live and walk according to the rules and regulations of the divine government in the universe. Sometimes the children of God suffer because they have violated the rules and regulations ordained by God and therefore receive God's discipline.

FIRST, SECOND, AND THIRD JOHN— THE FELLOWSHIP OF LIFE

The books of 1, 2 and 3 John are a supplement concerning the fellowship of life. When Christians are having problems or when the brothers and sisters in the church are having trouble among themselves, the reason is usually that the fellowship between them and the Lord or between them and other saints is not in a proper condition. Hence, there is the need to restore the fellowship of life.

JUDE—THE PROBLEM OF APOSTASY

Jude, the last of the supplementary books, mentions the problem of apostasy in the church. It shows us the situation and result of the apostasy that occurred among the children of God. This supplementary word gives us several warnings.

REVELATION—
THE ACCOMPLISHMENT OF GOD'S BUILDING

The last book of the New Testament is the book of Revelation. At the very beginning Revelation mentions seven lampstands, which are seven churches. Every local church is a lampstand. According to the Lord's view, the church is a lampstand, and Christ Himself is the lamp. When the New Jerusalem is manifested, it will be a big lampstand with Christ Himself as the lamp within. Therefore, every local church is a miniature lampstand, a miniature New Jerusalem, for Christ to shine forth. This is the manifestation of the fully built up church.

At the beginning of Revelation are the seven lampstands, at the end is a great city, and in the middle is a long section concerning God's judgment. God is always judging. He judges again and again to clear out all those who are not built into the church. Everyone who has not been regenerated and saved, who has not pursued spiritual growth, and who is against God's building will be judged. In the end God will judge Babylon, the totality of Satan's building. Recall that in the beginning we mentioned the two lines of building—the line of God's building and the line of Satan's building. In order to complete His building, God must judge Satan's building. In the end God's judgment will fall upon Babylon. Afterward, He will judge the great dragon, the ancient serpent, which is called the devil, and will cast him along with death into the lake of fire and brimstone. At this juncture the New Jerusalem will be manifested, and God's building will be completed.

THE LIGHT CONCERNING BUILDING SEEN
THROUGHOUT THE ENTIRE NEW TESTAMENT

If you put together all the light in the Bible concerning the
building of the church, you will clearly see that Christ was
God who became flesh, passed through death, resurrection,
and ascension, and in the Holy Spirit came into us, His believers, and regenerated us so that the Ark, which was made of
wood overlaid with gold, the mingling of divinity and humanity, might be enlarged to be the tabernacle, the church. We
who are the components of the church were formerly sinners,
but by believing in Jesus Christ we were justified by God and
transferred out of Adam into Christ. As we live in the Holy
Spirit, we are being conformed to the image of God's Son, and
by our coordination with one another we are becoming the
one Body of Christ. Although we still have the factors of
division in our flesh, all the divisive factors will be nullified if
we receive Christ and the cross. Furthermore, in the church
there is the need for the leading of mature ministers like
Paul. These are those who have passed through God's beating
and grinding, the cross's breaking, and the Spirit's constituting work and have become ministers for the building of the
church. When the church is under the leading of such ministers, the saints are delivered from the law and their own
works on the one hand, and on the other hand, they live in
Christ, take Christ as their life, and let Christ grow and be
formed in them. In this way the church experiences the real
building up to be the Body of Christ and the dwelling place of
God. Only such a church can be the man of the new creation,
the counterpart of Christ, and the warrior of God. Only such a
church knows the resurrection power of Christ and is being
conformed to the image of Christ in His death by such a
power. Hence, in such a church Christ has the first place in
all things, and the church enjoys all the riches in Christ.
Furthermore, we need to see that in such a church where
there is the practical building, there should be an atmosphere
of brotherly love, like Philemon's love toward Onesimus and
like the situation in the church in Philadelphia. Then the
church that appears in each locality is a lampstand, a small

model of the New Jerusalem, through which Christ shines forth.

Therefore, the church is like a lampstand. Christ is the lamp, and the light in the lamp is God Himself. In other words, God is in Christ, and Christ is in the church. The light is in the lamp, and the lamp is on the lampstand. This is exactly like the Ten Commandments being in the Ark and the Ark being in the tabernacle. It is always a matter of three layers. At the fullness of the times, the work of God throughout the ages will be accomplished. At that time, the twelve tribes of the Old Testament and the church, represented by the twelve apostles of the New Testament, will be joined together to become one entity, which will be the manifestation of the New Jerusalem in the universe. This is the consistent revelation throughout the entire New Testament.

Now we need to clearly see what kind of Christian we should be today to be according to God's heart's desire. May we as living stones be built together in the Spirit to become God's dwelling place in spirit, and may we be Christ's lampstands in this dark age in locality after locality so that the light of God in Christ as the lamp may shine forth from each locality until the appearance of the New Jerusalem. This is the accomplishment of God's eternal plan and goal through our aspiration and consecration. May God bestow His grace upon us.

CHAPTER EIGHT

THE PRACTICE OF THE BUILDING OF THE CHURCH

Scripture Reading: Matt. 16:15-18; Eph. 2:19-22; 3:17-21; 1 Pet. 2:4-5; 1 Cor. 3:9-12; Rom. 12:3-6; Eph. 4:11-12, 15-16; 1 Cor. 14:4-5, 12

We thank the Lord for bringing us through this series of messages. May the Lord bestow His grace upon us and give us the best conclusion to this subject. May He cause us to not only understand His revelation and see His vision but also to allow Him to take a real step among us to accomplish the work that He wishes to accomplish. In this message we will cover some specific matters that are closely related to the practice of the church.

The Bible may be divided into three sections. The first section, comprising the two ends of the Bible, shows us two corresponding pictures. The picture at the beginning reveals the building materials that God wants to have, and the picture at the end reveals how God builds these precious materials into a tabernacle to be His dwelling place in the universe.

The second section shows us that the Old Testament, from beginning to end, is centered on the tabernacle and the temple, both of which are types indicating that God will build all of His redeemed people into His habitation on the earth for the expression of His glory.

The third section shows us that when the Lord Jesus came to the earth in the New Testament, He was God entering into man, putting on humanity, and living among men. It was at this time that God pitched a living tabernacle among men. This living tabernacle was His body, the temple where He dwelt. One day the Jews killed and tore down the body of the Lord Jesus, but on the third day His body was resurrected. His resurrected body denotes not only Himself alone but also the thousands and thousands of people whom He regenerated in His resurrection. These regenerated ones have His life, and they also have Him living in them. Corporately, they are the church, which is the enlarged Body of the Lord, the tabernacle and the temple where God dwells. At the end of the Bible, the work of God throughout the ages is completed, and the completed New Jerusalem, the glorious city, appears as God's habitation in which God may dwell and through which God may be expressed. This is the picture that we have seen in the entire Bible.

In the previous message, we went through the entire New Testament in a concise way and considered it from the view of the matter of building to see how marvelous God's arrangement is. The New Testament begins by telling us that God became flesh and enlarged Himself among men to become the church and to be joined with the church. Subsequently, we see the churches being built up in various localities and the lampstands appearing in locality after locality so that Christ as the lamp can shine forth God as the light through the lampstands. Finally, at the end of the ages, the holy city New Jerusalem appears as a great lampstand. With a height of twelve thousand stadia (a stadium equals approximately six hundred feet), the New Jerusalem is quite high. Therefore, the holy city is like a tall lampstand. Christ is the lamp set upon the holy city, and God Himself is the light inside the lamp, shining Himself out through the lamp and the lampstand. The nations around shall walk in this light. This is the picture of the building in the Scriptures. It is a story of three layers—God being in Christ and Christ being in the church, which is typified by the Ten Commandments being in the Ark and the Ark being in the tabernacle. I believe that you all should be quite clear about this picture and this vision.

Now we will go on to see how we, the saved ones, can become the builded church. We will especially focus on the practical aspect. However, in many places we will still have to go back to touch the matter of the vision.

NEEDING TO BE DEALT WITH TO BE BUILT

Every person who has been saved, who loves the Lord, who pursues after Him, and who has seen God's vision will have the clear realization that to properly be a Christian he must be built together with his fellow Christians. Previously, we were sinners who belonged to the world and needed to be saved. Now that we have been saved, we need to take a further step to be built into the church. To be built does not mean that we merely pursue the Lord, love the Lord, and are spiritual but that we also commit ourselves into the hand of the Lord, allowing Him to do the work of trimming and dealing in us so that we may become material fit for God's dwelling place. This is similar to the building of a house. The materials may have been purchased, but before the actual building can begin, the craftsmen must do a considerable amount of work on the materials first. If they are dealing with stones, they must do some knocking, chiseling, and carving of designs. If they are handling lumber, they must do some sawing and planing so that the lumber will fit the required measurements. After the materials have been properly worked on, then they can be put together according to the blueprint and be built into a house. This is a very simple illustration.

Just as a builder buys the building materials, so God has bought and redeemed us with the blood of His Son to be materials for His building. Some of the materials are large, while others are small. Some are like stones, while others are like lumber. After obtaining the materials, God brings them to the church. On the one hand, the church is a home, but on the other hand, the church is a factory where God works. The first thing God does is to work on the materials with an ax, hammer, knife, and chisel. He cuts away the excess parts and planes the rough surfaces.

While we are under these kinds of dealings, we may be very troubled and may sometimes be full of complaints. Hence, some may begin to doubt and ask, "When we heard the gospel, we were told that after we were saved, we would have peace. So why is it that we have no peace now?" I remember when I was young and newly saved, I was very zealous to preach the gospel everywhere. One time I met a friend who was having difficulties, and I told him, "You have to believe in the Lord right away. You truly need the Lord. You are suffering so much, you are physically sick, and your situation is difficult. You can have peace only by believing in the Lord." Thank the Lord that he believed in the Lord and that the Lord was merciful toward him. He soon recovered from his sickness, his situation also improved, and he truly had joy and peace.

Some Christians are full of enjoyment when they first believe in the Lord. Soon afterward, however, they again experience trouble in their lives and changes in their circumstances, and their faith gradually wavers. Sometimes they would come and ask me, "Mr. Lee, the gospel that you preached to me was true in the beginning, but now it is no longer true. May I ask you why it is that the more I trust in the Lord and the more I pray, the more the difficulties increase? It seems that the Lord Jesus does not hear my prayers or solve my problems. What is the matter?" Then they would further question me, saying, "Could it be that the Lord in whom we have believed is not real?" I would say, "Of course He is real!" Then they would say, "Since He is real, how can He bear to see us suffer? If this is so, then is it true that our Lord does not have love?" Whenever they asked this, I was unable to answer them, and even I began to doubt. I thought that since it was so troublesome to believe in the Lord, perhaps we would be happier as unbelievers.

Sometimes I would go to some old preachers for help. They explained to me that God often has to discipline and chasten us because we make mistakes. At first I thought that this explanation was correct, because it seemed impossible for us children of God to never be wrong. Sometimes we are wrong in our attitude, and other times we are wrong in our words. Our God who is also our Father loves us, so He surely chastises us and disciplines us when we are wrong. Therefore, we should take His discipline willingly.

Gradually, however, I discovered that sometimes He would chastise me when I had done nothing wrong. Sometimes I had obviously done nothing wrong, and my condition before God was very good, yet problems still came to me repeatedly. Again I was perplexed. I asked myself whether or not God would discipline and chastise me even if I had not sinned. I could not understand this. At that time I was altogether groping in the dark since I had never heard a message concerning building and had no proper person to help me.

After groping in the dark for many years, the Lord gradually led me to know something concerning the church and to see the vision of the building. Furthermore, I experienced coordinating with various kinds of saints among the brothers and sisters, such as the co-workers and elders, the responsible ones of the home meetings and group meetings, the experienced ones, and the younger ones. I saw that all the saints had to serve in one accord and in coordination to be a proper church. Gradually, I realized that to have this kind of coordination, the Lord's dealing is needed. We need to be dealt with even if we have not erred in any matter. This is similar to the way a house is built. Lumber from Chinese juniper trees is very good. It has neither knots nor blemishes. However, if you measured the pieces of lumber, you would discover that some are too long. Thus, you would need to saw off some parts to make them suitable to be used. If the lumber had any feeling, it might say to the carpenter, "Why are you cutting me? Is it because I did something wrong? Do I have any knots or blemishes? Do I have other problems?" If I were the carpenter, I would tell the lumber, "It is not a matter of whether or not you have made a mistake. Look at how long you are. I want to make you into a doorpost, which is only eight feet high, but you are half a foot too long. What do you think I should do? I need to work on you by cutting and sawing off a piece of you, or else you will be completely useless in the building." This piece of juniper wood would have no choice but to suffer the pain and allow the carpenter to deal with it as he sees fit.

I use this simple illustration to speak about the building of the church. When we were saved, the element of God as pure gold was added into us, the earthen vessels. However, God still wants us to be transformed into pearls and precious stones. Today technology has advanced to such an extent that diamonds can be artificially produced through intense heat and great pressure. We know that the elementary composition of diamonds is the same as that of common coal, but after going through a long process of being under intense heat and great pressure, the ordinary coal is transformed into a precious diamond. In the same manner, we who are common materials like lumps of clay need to be transformed if we want to be built together in the church. Hence, transformation becomes a big problem to us.

This matter of transformation is not up to us. It is altogether a matter of the Lord's leading. When we were first saved, due to the Lord's attracting, we pursued Him, loved Him, fellowshipped constantly with Him, lived in Him, and were willing to give ourselves to Him. As a result, we felt very sweet within. However, for some unknown reason, it seemed that after a while an invisible hand mysteriously came upon us, bringing sufferings. Sometimes the sufferings came gradually, and sometimes they came all at once. We had no way of escape. What kind of story is this? This is the work of God. Our sufferings, which are all permitted and measured by God, put us into the furnace of trials. Sometimes the sufferings are so heavy that it seems that we can no longer bear them, and we may even ask for death. We do not realize that in burning and pressing us, God's intention is to remake us so that we would be gradually transformed to be suitable for building. Such a transformation is not to make us spiritual for others to appreciate. Rather, it is to make us able to be coordinated, mingled, and built together with the other members. This is the ultimate goal of God's work.

NEEDING TO CONSIDER THE BUILDING OF
THE CHURCH AS AN IMPORTANT MATTER

At the Lord's table and on other occasions I have often heard the brothers and sisters thanking and praising God with the words of Ephesians 2:19, saying, "O God, formerly we were strangers and sojourners, but we thank and praise You that now we are fellow citizens with the saints and members of the household of God." However, they usually end their thanksgivings and praises there. They do not notice that verse 20 goes on to say, "Being built upon the foundation of the apostles and prophets." We should not think that after we are saved it is sufficient to enter into God's kingdom and God's house to be God's children and to become spiritual material. We still need to be built so that we can reach the goal of God's calling.

What a pity that this matter has been so neglected among God's children! I have been a Christian from my youth, and I have yet to hear a message concerning God's building. Our hymnal contains hymns that were selected from over ten thousand hymns and may be considered a collection of the best Christian hymns. Today, however, when we release messages concerning the building, every time we want to choose a hymn for this topic, we can only shake our heads and sigh. We cannot find a hymn in our hymnal that contains the word *building,* much less find a hymn whose topic is the building. We can easily find hymns on salvation, consecration, loving the Lord, pursuing the Lord, being filled with Christ, being filled with the Holy Spirit, and bearing the cross. However, we cannot find one hymn that says, "Lord, I want to be built, and I need to be built. If I am not built, I cannot reach Your goal!" All of God's children need to see how much this matter of the building of the church is neglected among the children of God.

Thank the Lord that recently, after returning to Taipei from my visits abroad, I saw many brothers and sisters in the church in Taipei consecrating themselves for the building and receiving the laying on of hands by the elders. Among them were some older ones and also some younger ones. Some had been saved for a long time, and others had been saved only recently. I felt very happy in my heart. When I saw the brothers and sisters giving their testimonies and reading their consecration declarations in the meetings, I bowed my head and worshiped the Lord, saying, "Thank and praise the Lord that today in the church there are people who can speak concerning the building!" In all my years of service to the Lord, I have heard countless numbers of saints consecrate themselves to the Lord and speak a great deal on consecration, but

I never heard one mention a word about building. However, within the past two months, I have personally heard many brothers and sisters spontaneously say in their consecration, "O Lord, now I know that You are a God without a home. You cannot find a resting place on the earth. Thus, You need to build a spiritual house. You are saving people that they may be material for the building. By Your mercy I am also a piece of material. I want to consecrate myself to You for Your building."

This is a wonderful thing. I thank and praise the Lord that today something has finally been imparted into some of God's children. We should not despise this aspect of God's work, nor should we depreciate the desire of God's children for this matter. I deeply believe that in these last days God will recover this important matter of building and instill it into His children in a definite way. How I thank and praise God for this conference. In the past eleven years in Taipei, we have had a total of thirteen conferences, including the present one. However, none of the past conferences can compare with the present one in the consistency of the attendance. There has been almost no decrease in attendance from the beginning to the end. Furthermore, I can clearly sense that the absorbing power of the audience is very strong. The words that are being spoken flow out effortlessly, like a great amount of water passing through a pipe by being compressed at one end and drawn off at the other end. I am convinced that this is God's work in the last age. Although our spiritual condition is still immature and does not amount to much before God and men, when I see the work of God among His children in these days, I cannot but lift up my spirit and worship God. We must acknowledge that because of His mercy and through His word, God has caused an exceedingly great light to shine among us, showing us that His eternal purpose is to build a glorious church for His glorious Son Christ, who transcends everything. We the saved ones are the material for this building. We are not only saved, are not only spiritual, and are not only loving the Lord, but we are also being built together to be the glorious church. Is there anything else in the universe that is more blessed or pleasing to God and more satisfying to God's heart's desire?

In the past I have met many of God's children who were full of feelings for themselves and who cared only for their own welfare, security, future, and benefit in the present life. When I was young and was beginning to serve the Lord, I frequently gave messages telling Christians to love the Lord. One time someone stood up in the meeting and asked me, "Mr. Lee, if a person only believes in the Lord but does not love the Lord, is he saved or not?" I said, "Since you have believed in the Lord, you should love the Lord." He said, "It is easy for me to believe in the Lord, but it is difficult for me to love the Lord. If this is the case, am I still saved?" This question was so difficult for me to answer! I then said to him, "You should love the Lord after you are saved. Otherwise, you will not receive the reward when the Lord returns." He said, "I do not care whether or not I receive a reward. It does not even matter to me if I do not enter into heaven. I will be satisfied to merely stand at the door of heaven and not have to go to hell." This incident occurred in 1935 in a meeting in Tientsin. Many people in their concept and feeling are altogether for their own well-being and security. This is truly pitiful!

Today in His mercy the Lord has opened the eyes of our heart to show us that God has a most glorious and exceedingly great need in the universe. He needs a living house, a living temple, and a living habitation on the earth. He saves people because He wants them to not only love Him and pursue spiritual things but also to commit themselves into His hand to be worked on by Him under His burning and pressure so that they may be delivered from their individual spirituality, peculiar traits, and independence and thereby be built together in the church to become the glorious dwelling place of God! This building is the unique goal in God's eternal purpose and plan.

Over twenty years ago I read a book specifically on consecration. In that book the writer said that the Lord saves us so that He can work on us and deal with us to make us into pieces of treasure to display in heaven in the future, just as treasures are displayed in the houses of great families or in

the palaces of kings for people to admire and praise. Therefore, we should not be afraid of sufferings through afflictions.
Rather, we should present ourselves into the Lord's hand and
allow Him to deal with us, burn us, and press us so that we
would gradually be transformed into precious treasures and
be placed in heaven for display. How honorable and glorious
that would be! When I read that book, I thought that this concept was very logical, and I even related it to others. Later,
however, I read the Bible again, and no matter how much I
read it, I could not find any passage telling us that there will
be pieces of precious stones put on display in heaven. Instead,
after reading the Bible again and again, I discovered that the
issue of God's work throughout the ages is the building of
the transformed materials, the pearls and precious stones,
into a holy city.

NEEDING TO BE DELIVERED FROM INDEPENDENCE

We must continually see that God's desire is that we
would be those who are being built. Perhaps some will ask,
"How can we be those who are being built?" First, we must be
delivered from our independence and learn to be joined to
others. Consider a house for example. Every piece of wood in a
house is connected to other pieces of wood that are above it,
below it, on its left, and on its right. Not one piece stands alone.
In the same manner, we Christians need to learn to be joined
to the brothers and sisters around us. No matter how different our tastes, personalities, and views are, we still have to be
joined together. This joining together will take away some of
our freedom. Some brothers and sisters have brought this
matter up with me. One of them said to me, "Being joined
together surely has its good points." After hearing such a
remark, I immediately knew what he intended to say next, so
I said it for him: "But it also has its bad points." He said, "You
are altogether right." Then I asked him, "What are the bad
points?" He said, "The first bad point is that there is no freedom. When I am by myself and I feel to go and preach the
gospel, I can do so freely. However, if someone is joined to me,
then I am restricted in many ways." I asked him, "What is so
bad about this?" He replied, "When I act alone, I can keep

everything secret, but once I am joined to someone, that one will even know how much rice I ate. How inconvenient this is!"

I have discovered something quite amazing in Europe and in the United States. People in the West are very afraid of one thing—being unable to keep a secret. They are very afraid of people knowing their private matters. While I was visiting the West, I would sometimes get letters. If I was talking with guests in the living room, the host would hand me the letters with the back side up. At first I thought that this was a great courtesy, but gradually I discovered that the host's real intention was to guard my privacy by not letting the guests know where the letter had come from. Please do not blame me for referring to these kinds of matters. The problem with many brothers and sisters in regard to the building of the church is that they are not willing to let others know about their affairs and therefore cannot have proper fellowship with the brothers and sisters around them. They can only serve alone and are not willing to put aside their peculiarities.

NEEDING TO BE DELIVERED FROM BEING INSEPARABLY JOINED

There is also another kind of problem regarding the building. Some brothers and sisters are so joined together that they cannot be separated, similar to the way flesh and skin grow together and cannot be separated. We human beings are very difficult to manage. Either we cannot be joined with others, or once we are joined together, we cannot be separated. This is so difficult! In the past I have met at least three or four pairs of brothers who were inseparable in this way. Whenever they came together, they would whisper with each other as if they had some secrets that could not be told to others. You could not pull them apart no matter what. Please forgive me for speaking in very plain words. I have been in this "business" of building the church for over thirty years. When a master carpenter obtains a piece of wood, he can readily detect its problems. With only one look he can tell where the knots and blemishes are. It is the same in the process of building God's children. An expert, with only one look, immediately knows where the problems are. Nothing can be hidden from him. When someone says, "I cannot be joined to others," then we should be clear that this one has problems with the building. If someone says, "I can be joined to others," then we must not believe this one too quickly. We must see whether or not he can be separated after he has been joined. If he cannot be disconnected after being joined, then this will be a problem. That kind of joining cannot stand the test. In the building of the church, the brothers and sisters should be able to be separated from others as well as joined to others. When they need to be joined, they should be able to be joined, and when they need to be separated, they should be able to be separated. In this way there will be no problems.

THE BUILDING BEING THE YARDSTICK AND THE TEST FOR ALL SPIRITUAL MATTERS

Finally, I would like to seriously remind God's children that the building is the yardstick and the test for all spiritual matters. We must use the building as a yardstick to test whether the spiritual condition of the brothers and sisters is proper or not. If the more spiritual you are, the more independent you become, or the less able you are to be joined to others, then surely your spirituality is questionable. If the more you love the Lord, the more you feel that you are higher and better than others and the more you like to condemn others, then there is something wrong with your loving the Lord. Clearly, we human beings are not so simple.

I know some believers who have learned the lesson of prayer well, but strangely, although they pray so much, they cannot be joined to others. The more they pray, the less they are joined to others. Eventually, they can pray only by themselves. They form a habit in which they must find a quiet room, lock the door, and solemnly kneel down and pray. The more these ones pray, the more they sense the presence of the Lord, and the more they enter into fellowship with the Lord. It is difficult to say whether this kind of prayer is good or not. However, one thing is for sure—ultimately, every person who prays in this manner will not pray with others and will even stop attending the prayer meeting of the church. If you ask such a person why he prays in this manner, he will use the Scriptures to prove his case, saying, "Have you not read about how the Lord Jesus went to the garden of Gethsemane to pray? First, He and the disciples left the crowd and came to the deserted garden of Gethsemane. Then He took three of the disciples aside and left the others behind. However, this was not enough, so finally, leaving the three disciples, He went forward a little to pray alone before God. Only this is real prayer." If you ask him why he does not attend the prayer meeting, he will again give you many reasons, saying, "Have you noticed what kinds of people are in the meeting? All of them are old ladies who have been saved only recently and old men who are in their seventies. When they pray, their voices are so soft and their prayers are so long. Their prayers put me to sleep. How could I pray there?" He will argue so much for only one principle, the principle of being freed from the crowd to go forward a little to the place where the Lord Jesus prayed alone. He also may give you another illustration, saying, "Look at the story in the Old Testament. When Moses went to meet God at Mount Sinai, his first step was to take Aaron with him and to leave the people of Israel behind. His second step was to leave Aaron at the foot of the mountain and to go alone to see God on the mountaintop. Therefore, to truly come before God we must be alone."

We may have nothing to say when we meet this kind of brother. However, we should not laugh at him. This is a problem that we frequently encounter in the church. Such brothers do not realize that the Lord Jesus did not always pray alone in the garden of Gethsemane. Instead, He spent much time being mingled with the disciples. Similarly, Moses was on the mountain for only forty days at the most, while most of the time he was being mingled with the people of Israel. These brothers who think that they are following the pattern of prayer set by the Lord Jesus and Moses have never mingled with God's children.

Not only can prayer be a problem, but spiritual gifts can also become a problem in the building of the church. Many brothers and sisters admire spiritual gifts, and the church needs them as well. However, many brothers and sisters seem

able to be joined to others before their spiritual gifts are manifested, but once they become somewhat useful in the church
and once their gifts have been manifested a little, then they
want to be alone and not be associated with others. Therefore,
the building is a great balance. If you pray to such an extent
that you become independent and cannot pray with others,
then you must immediately be balanced by the building. To
pray is right, but you cannot go to the extreme. You need to be
balanced. Similarly, spiritual gifts are right, but if the gifts
cause you to be unable to coordinate with the brothers and
sisters, then you have swerved toward the extreme. Thus, we
need the light of the building to balance us.

Once we have the personal experience, we will realize that
only by being built can we be truly spiritual. Furthermore, we
will realize that only when we are built with others can we
have the full knowledge and experience of Christ, which far
surpasses the knowledge and experience that we have when
we pursue the Lord alone. I am not annulling the individual
aspect of the Christian life. However, we must realize that the
truth in the Bible always has two sides, like a cake. The
Christian life has an aspect of being alone, and it also has an
aspect of being coordinated with others. It has an individual
aspect and also a corporate aspect. When we want to fully
enjoy Christ, taste the riches of the Lord's love, and feel the
rich presence of the Lord, then we must come to the church.
For example, when we sing the hymns, we often sense an
especially rich flavor. One absolutely cannot obtain that kind
of rich flavor while singing hymns alone at home with the
door shut. In another example, suppose the responsible brothers and sisters in a home meeting are in coordination and in
one accord. There are no spiritual giants among them, and
there are no especially gifted ones or talented ones. Yet when
they preach the gospel, they are able to bring more people
to salvation than the gifted ones can. Moreover, the number of
attendees in their meetings is very large, and the spirit in the
meetings is very strong. The reason that they have God's
blessing and presence is because they are willing to be balanced by the building.

Finally, what the Lord wants today is not a church that

seems to be spiritual but is not being built up. What the Lord wants is a church that is both spiritual and balanced by the building. Only such a builded church can be the tabernacle and dwelling place of God for God and man to have rest together.

CHAPTER NINE

THE RESPONSE TO THE BUILDING
OF THE CHURCH

Scripture Reading: 1 Chron. 29:3-9; Ezra 1:1-6; 3:1-3, 8-13;
Hag. 1:2, 4; Rom. 12:1, 5

God's eternal intention is to build for Himself a glorious dwelling place, a glorious church, among His saved ones through the life of His Son. Therefore, all the work that God is doing upon us who have been saved is for us to be built together to become a spiritual house in which He can live.

I feel that we cannot merely listen to God's word and see God's vision yet not have any response or action before God. In the Bible—whether in the Old Testament concerning the tabernacle and the temple or the New Testament concerning the building of the church—God first reveals His heart's desire to His people, showing them a spiritual vision that they might know that He wants to do something exceedingly glorious in the universe. Then His people respond and take action before God, and as a result, His intention is accomplished among them.

THE RESPONSE OF THE PEOPLE OF ISRAEL
TO THE BUILDING IN THE OLD TESTAMENT

Before the people of Israel built the tabernacle, Moses led them to the foot of Mount Sinai, where God revealed to Moses the heavenly pattern in a vision. Then Moses told the Israelites the vision that he had seen. After the whole congregation knew God's desire, they immediately responded by committing themselves to Moses and doing their best to offer to God all of the things that they had received of Him. They rose up as one man and coordinated together, each one doing his part to build the tabernacle of God in one accord. Later, when the Israelites built the temple, their response to God's desire was even stronger and more glorious. David was perhaps the first one to respond. Although he did not personally build the temple, because he had set his affection on the temple, he used all of his effort to prepare the materials for the temple of God, even in the midst of the hardships of war. Besides this, he also offered his entire private treasure of gold and silver, which included three thousand talents of gold from the gold of Ophir and seven thousand talents of refined silver. More- over, he said to the congregation of the Israelites, "Who will offer willingly, consecrating himself today to Jehovah?" After David sounded the call, the leaders of the fathers' houses, the leaders of the tribes of Israel, the captains of thousands, and the captains of hundreds with the overseers of the king's work all responded and offered themselves absolutely and willingly. They gave five thousand talents and ten thousand darics of gold, ten thousand talents of silver, eighteen thou- sand talents of bronze, and one hundred thousand talents of iron for the service of the house of God. In addition, they offered many precious stones. Then the people rejoiced because they had offered willingly to God with their whole heart, and David also rejoiced with great joy. Therefore, when the building of the temple was completed, the temple was filled with glory.

Regrettably, after a short time the people of Israel became desolate, and as a result the temple was destroyed and the people of Israel were taken captive to foreign lands. When- ever they remembered the desolation of the temple, they were filled with sorrow and sighing. They hoped that one day they would see the temple rebuilt. During their captivity, in the first year of the reign of Darius, who was made king over the Chaldeans, Daniel read the Scriptures written by the prophet Jeremiah and understood that the number of years for the completion of the desolation of Jerusalem would be seventy. Thus, he set his face toward God to seek Him in prayer, sup- plication, and confession of sins with fasting and sackcloth and ashes. God then sent Gabriel to Daniel in a vision to promise him that the people of Israel would recover the holy temple and the holy city (Dan. 9). We know that before this time, Daniel prayed to God in his house (with the windows open toward Jerusalem) three times daily on his knees (6:10). I believe that in his prayers he must have asked God to quickly recover the building of the holy temple and the holy city.

Thank God that in the first year of King Cyrus (at that time Daniel was already quite old), God, in order to fulfill His promise, stirred up the spirit of Cyrus, king of Persia. Although Cyrus was a Gentile king, he was used by God to accomplish God's will. He made a proclamation throughout his entire kingdom and put it in writing, saying, "All the kingdoms of the earth has Jehovah the God of heaven given to me; and He has charged me to build Him a house in Jerusalem, which is in Judah. Whoever there is among you of all His people, may His God be with him; and let him go up to Jerusalem, which is in Judah, and let him build the house of Jehovah the God of Israel—He is God—who is in Jerusalem." Furthermore, he said, "Everyone who is left, in whatever place he sojourns, let the men of his place support him with silver and with gold and with goods and with cattle, besides the freewill offering for the house of God, which is in Jerusalem" (Ezra 1:2-4). After he sounded the call, immediately there was a great response among the Israelites. Verses 5 through 8 say, "The heads of the fathers' houses of Judah and Benjamin and the priests and the Levites rose up, even everyone whose spirit God had stirred up to go up to build the house of Jehovah, which is in Jerusalem. And all those around them strengthened their hands with vessels of silver, with gold, with goods, and with cattle and with precious things, besides all that was offered willingly. Also King Cyrus brought out the vessels of the house of Jehovah...and had them enumerated to Sheshbazzar the prince of Judah." Thus, the people of Israel traveled in groups from Babylon to Jerusalem. When they arrived at Jerusalem, they gathered together as one man and endeavored in one accord to rebuild the temple.

Before rebuilding the temple, they rebuilt the altar, because the altar was for offering sacrifices. This meant that before the building of the temple could begin, there had to be an act of consecration. The main reason for the consecration of God's people was not that they would offer their goods but that they would place themselves in the hand of God. We can see from the record in the book of Ezra that the glory of the situation at that time apparently surpassed the glory of the situation at the time when the temple was first built. When the builders laid the foundation of the temple on the original site, they set the priests in their apparel with trumpets and the Levites, the sons of Asaph, with cymbals to praise God. They sang to one another in praising and giving thanks to God. All the people shouted with a great shout, and the old men who had seen the first house wept with a loud voice, having been greatly stirred up in their emotions. The stirring and excitement within the Israelites at that time surpassed their excitement in the past. It was truly an unprecedented event. Because they had passed through the painful experience and lesson of captivity, they could not help having such a strong reaction after returning to their own land and seeing the rebuilding of the temple.

THE RECOVERY OF GOD'S BUILDING WORK
IN THE CHURCH

Now I would like to say something about our present condition. On the day of Pentecost when the Spirit of God descended and when the church was first begun on the earth, the condition of the church was truly glorious, like the condition of the temple at its beginning after the people of Israel had built it. Not long afterward, however, this glorious church was damaged by the enemy and became desolate, like what happened in the tragedy of the captivity of the Israelites in the Old Testament. Since then, those who belong to God, who love God with a pure heart, and who sympathize with God's desire have been sighing, saying, "Alas, the days of glory have passed! The glorious church has been torn down!" They have been expectantly waiting to see the glorious church rebuilt.

If we read church history, we will see that the goal of God's work on the earth is to recover His church. Apparently, He is recovering portions of the truth and light or portions of grace and glory. Actually, however, if you look at the whole picture, you will see that His ultimate goal is to recover His glorious church. If you have been paying attention to the matter of the church, particularly during the last thirty to forty years, you have seen that what God has been doing among His children is recovering in a strong way the matter of the church, not only in its spiritual aspect but also in its practical aspect. If you collected the worthy spiritual writings put out during the past forty years—whether biographies of individuals, histories of the church, or records of the establishment of churches in various localities—and if you studied them comprehensively, then you would have to praise the Lord. You would have to acknowledge that during this period of time God has done a sufficient work of preparation for the recovery of the building of His glorious church.

THE FEELING OF THE MINISTERS OF GOD'S WORD TODAY

Not only is God continually doing this kind of work, but countless saints are also frequently supplicating, praying, waiting, and sighing in the presence of God, hoping to soon see with their own eyes the manifestation of a real, solid, built up, and glorious church. Furthermore, some who are ministers of God's word and who speak for God and serve as His mouthpiece have touched the feeling in God's heart through their habitual living before God and their intimate fellowship with Him. Thus, they express such feelings in the messages that they release to God's children. During the past thirty years, whenever the leading co-workers among us stood up to speak for God, the Holy Spirit gave us the feeling and inclination to not stay away from the matter of the church. Many times we who serve as God's mouthpiece come together before the Lord to seek His intention. We ask, "What does the Lord want to do in this age? What way is He taking? What kinds of words and messages does He want to release through us?" At these times we always have the same feeling, which is that God wants to recover the building of the church.

No doubt, we should preach the gospel and release the truth. We should also lead the believers to love the Lord, be zealous for Him, draw near to Him, and fellowship with Him.

Furthermore, we must show the believers that the Lord is our
life and that He mingles Himself with us so that we may be
transformed, become full-grown, and arrive at the measure of
the stature of the fullness of Christ. However, within us is a
heavier and deeper feeling. We feel that we do not have much
to say unless we speak about the concrete manifestation of
the church on the earth and the building of the church. When
we release messages on other matters, we sense that there is
no echo within and that our speaking misses the mark and
is not powerful. If we do not go in the direction of the church,
we will feel that we have not carried out the ministry that
God has committed to us. Moreover, our work will never reach
God's goal or satisfy God's heart's desire.

Around 1930, there were only a few of us who were serving
the Lord, and almost every one of us fell into various kinds of
trials. We each had our own difficulties, and almost every one
had some kind of sickness. Stomach trouble and tuberculosis
were very common among us, and I myself was no exception.
Some also had high blood pressure and heart disease. The
situation then was truly difficult. In spite of this, we still
preached the word, wrote articles, and conversed with others
every day. We often said to one another, "We may not have too
many days to live on the earth!" The older brother among
us was only in his thirties. I clearly remember that one day he
was sitting on a rocking chair, and while he was rocking,
he said, "Brothers, whether we have lung trouble, stomach
trouble, high blood pressure, or heart disease, the 'stop' is in
the hand of the Lord. You know that I have stomach trouble
and also heart disease. Frequently when I am preaching, I
have to press my abdomen against the pulpit in front of me,
due to my stomachache. Sometimes at the end of my speaking, the color of my face turns green, because my heart is
beating too fast. The first thing I do after I end my preaching
is to lie down on a bed to rest. I often tell myself that perhaps
this time would be my 'stop,' once I lie down. Every time after
I finish preaching, I am definitely prepared to 'stop' anytime.
My funeral arrangements are always ready. But up to now,
brothers, I have not stopped. Therefore, whether I stop or not,
my stopping is in the hand of the Lord." We then asked him,

"Does this mean that we who serve the Lord will always live a little longer regardless of the condition of our health?" He said, "It is not so. Many of those who speak for God have died young." We then asked, "What then does this mean?" He said, "Brothers, in the past many Bible expositors have expressed their thoughts in writing, saying that the signs that have been manifested in the present age all indicate that the Lord Jesus is coming back soon. Most people agree that in principle the Lord is coming back soon. However, I cannot believe that the Lord Jesus would come back right now."

When we heard this, we were puzzled. How did he jump from the topic of stomach trouble and heart disease to the topic of the Lord's return? None of us understood what he meant. After he saw our expressions, he went on and said, "Brothers, according to the Bible expositors, the Lord Jesus is returning soon. Furthermore, according to our health, it seems that we are not going to live much longer. However, I continue to sense within me that the glorious church of God has still not been built, and the burden in our spirit has still not been released. We have been speaking for God for more than ten years, but I have discovered that the more we speak, the heavier and greater the burden is within. I absolutely believe that this is a very serious matter, indicating that we still need to remain on the earth for quite a long time in order to release the burden within us. What is this burden? This burden is to tell God's children that in the last days of this age, God definitely will recover His church!"

He also said, "Brothers, please observe the present, real situation of Christianity in the East and in the West. Everywhere there are Christians who are zealous in preaching the gospel. There are many missions that send missionaries to the frontier to spread the gospel. Some are sent to South Africa and others to the interior of China. Remember, however, that although they have preached the gospel so much and have saved so many souls, God has not yet obtained a glorious church! Furthermore, ever since the Brethren were raised up a hundred years ago, many have spoken specifically about the secrets of being spiritual, beginning with consecration, and many of God's children have consecrated themselves to God. Brother Andrew Murray spoke about fellowship with the Lord as well as the indwelling Christ and the indwelling Spirit. After that, Mrs. Penn-Lewis spoke about dying with the Lord, and after her, someone else received special knowledge concerning resurrection. They all conveyed these spiritual matters to God's children, but where can we see the church?"

Then he went on to say, "Today there are a good number of authoritative scholars who know the Bible and can interpret the truth. Bible colleges for the training of Bible students and special books on Bible exposition have proliferated and are innumerable. However, I would like to ask where the church is. Today there are quite a few magazines and books published in Christianity, but how many articles in these publications specifically speak of God's desire to build a glorious church on the earth in a weighty and accurate way?"

After analyzing the situation, he told us, "Brothers, I do not know how you feel, but I am continually bearing a burden within, and the burden is growing heavier and heavier. My burden is to release messages on the building of the church to God's children. I hope to continually show God's children that God's eternal desire is to obtain a builded church in His Son. The reason God wants us to preach the gospel and save sinners is that we may gain material for the building of the church. The reason God wants us to love the Lord, consecrate ourselves to Him, pursue spirituality, and grow unto maturity is that we may be transformed to be fit for the Lord's use to build His church. I believe that you also have the same feeling within you, because today we are serving in coordination and in the same flow."

After I heard those words that day, immediately there was a response within me. I told the elder brother in a definite way, "I also have the same feeling within me!" At that time we clearly felt and deeply believed that no matter how much opposition we would encounter, no matter what the situation would be, no matter what our condition and that of the world would be, the Lord would still keep us on the earth. He would still keep us on the earth because we still needed to carry out the ministry that had been committed to us by God and to accomplish the glorious work of God. We wanted to see the glorious church of God recovered and rebuilt on the earth in the last days. When we read the book of Ezra together, we especially noticed the matter of how the Israelites recovered the temple. We all understood that this picture tells us that after God's church passes through a period of desolation, there will surely be a fullness of the times. When that time comes, God's church will be rebuilt.

I hope that you would not misunderstand. We absolutely do not intend to speak only about the church and neglect other spiritual matters. We will still actively preach the gospel and thoroughly present the truth, and we will also lead many to pursue spirituality. However, we feel that within us is a heavier burden. Whenever we have the opportunity to thoroughly speak on matters concerning the church—such as the content of the church, the riches of the church, the measure of the stature of the church, the way of the church, the ground of the church, the expression of the church, and the building of the church—our spirit leaps and feels satisfied, the burden within us is discharged, and our whole being feels light. This is an amazing thing!

I would like to seriously tell you that we few brothers who were there at that time are still on the earth today. Some of us are still releasing messages concerning the church, while some have been put into prison for the sake of the church and are still praying continually. This is a living testimony! This is just like the situation in the ancient times when the people of Israel were in captivity, yet people such as Daniel who were in the land of captivity still prayed facing Jerusalem. Although the brothers in prison have physically lost their freedom and cannot say much or do much, they are praying day and night. I believe that they are praying for God to recover the building of the church!

THE RESPONSE AND ACTION WE NEED TO HAVE TODAY

In this conference we have specifically spoken concerning the building of the church. We feel that the Holy Spirit has given this word a strong confirmation and that the spirit of the saints has had a strong response. I absolutely believe that in these eight or nine days many have seen what the center of

God's glorious vision is, what the meaning of human life is, and what God's eternal purpose and the goal of the living and service of God's children are. Furthermore, many saints have been praying and looking to the Lord behind the scenes. Therefore, I would like to ask you what our response should be and what action we should take. We need consecration! Consecration should be our response to God's building and the action that we take for God's building. We should commit ourselves into God's hand without any reservation. I would ask you to make a firm and determined indication of your response before God! May God accept and bless!

CHAPTER TEN

AUTHORITY, ORDER, AND BUILDING

Scripture Reading: Rev. 21:23; 1:20; Matt. 18:15-20; Rom. 12:3-11; Eph. 4:11-13, 15-16

Thank the Lord that in His abundant grace He has led us to the last message of this series. I am full of joy regarding the atmosphere of this conference. The Lord has not only revealed to us His vision of the building but has also begun a marvelous work in our hearts.

A few days ago we reached such a high peak in our spirit through the message that we all fervently responded to this glorious vision. I felt within that I should lead us all to come before God to make a specific indication of our response, that is, to formally and solemnly commit ourselves into the Lord's hand in the church. Thank the Lord that we have realized that with such a vision in front of us, we need to consecrate ourselves. This indicates that our hearts have definitely been moved by the Holy Spirit to such an extent that we are willing to commit ourselves into the Lord's hand to meet the need of the glorious building. I deeply believe that the Lord will accept our consecration.

In this message, standing on the ground of consecration, I would like to go on further and speak a more specific word to those who have consecrated themselves.

THE SMALL LAMPSTANDS AND
THE GREAT LAMPSTAND IN REVELATION

If we do not have the vision of the Lord in our reading of the Bible, then we will not be able to see its wonderful points, nor will we be able to see its emphasis. For example, in an earlier message we saw how the first two chapters of Genesis

correspond with the last two chapters of Revelation. I believe
that a great number of us had not seen such a vision in the
past, even though we may have read through the Bible several times. However, now through God's enlightenment and
revelation we have discovered the hidden treasures of the
Bible. When I was young and newly saved, I read through
Revelation once and felt that it was a very difficult book
because there were many places that I did not understand.
Later, someone told me that this book consists of prophecies
concerning the things that will take place throughout the
ages. This greatly stirred up my interest. Thus, I tried my
best to collect commentaries on Revelation for my reference.
Nearly all of these books merely explained the meanings of
the seven seals, the seven bowls, and the seven trumpets.
Some of the interpretations were almost nonsensical. Some
said that the locusts in Revelation are today's airplanes
and that the frogs are tanks on the earth. If you read those
expositions of the Bible, you will find that such strange expla-
nations are innumerable. If you lack the light of the truth and
do not know the principles of interpreting the Bible, then you
may think that these kinds of exposition are very meaningful
and may even be moved by them. In the end, however, you will
not know where you are.

By the Lord's mercy we have gradually received some revelation and knowledge concerning God's eternal purpose.
Therefore, we have begun to realize that God's intention is to
come into us through His Son to be our life and to mingle with
us as one entity for His expression. Furthermore, His desire
is to build us who have received God as life into a glorious
vessel to be His dwelling place and the Body of His Son,
which is also the bride of the Lamb. When we see this vision,
it becomes a yardstick, a standard, and a great light in our
reading of the Bible. Thus, when we come to the Bible to study
the prophecies, we can know precisely what they mean, and
we no longer have to look at them according to the common
interpretations of theology. When we see this vision, we
become more and more clear in our understanding of the book
of Revelation.

If we compare the beginning and the end of Revelation,

just as we compared the beginning and the end of the Bible, we will discover new light. At the end of Revelation, there is a holy city. This holy city is not a two-dimensional plane but a cube. It does not have two dimensions only—the length and the breadth, but it has a third dimension as well—the height. Moreover, its length, breadth, and height are equal, each measuring approximately 1,364 miles. Another special feature of the city is that it needs no artificial light or natural light because it is illuminated by the glory of God. God Himself is the light of the city. (In His nature, God is love and light. Love denotes the nature of God's essence, and light denotes the nature of God's expression. God in Himself is love, and when He is expressed, He is light.) In the holy city New Jerusalem, this light, which is God, shines out through the lamp, which is Christ the Lamb. If we read Revelation 21 carefully, we will find that the throne of God and of the Lamb is at the center of the city on a high peak. Therefore, this city, which is a cube, is like a huge lampstand. The walls around the city are clear as crystal, like a great glass lampshade, diffusing and shining forth the light of the city. The nations around the city walk in this light. Thus, this city, the New Jerusalem, is a huge lampstand in the midst of the surrounding nations. This lampstand has Christ as its lamp and God as the light in the lamp.

At the beginning of Revelation the matter of the lampstand is also mentioned. However, at the beginning there are several lampstands, seven in all, and they are small, not big. These seven lampstands are the lampstands in Ephesus, Smyrna, Pergamos, Thyatira, Sardis, Philadelphia, and Laodicea. At the end of Revelation there is only one great lampstand—the city of the New Jerusalem. With regard to time, the seven lampstands at the beginning exist in the present age, while the one at the end exists in eternity. With regard to location, the seven small lampstands at the beginning are found in different localities, while the great one at the end is found in the new heaven and new earth. The lampstands at the beginning and the end may be different in size, but regardless of whether they are great or small, they all have Christ as the lamp and God as the light within the lamp.

Some Bible readers have an inaccurate understanding of this matter. They think that each local church is a shining lamp. However, this is somewhat different from what the Bible says. Strictly speaking, each local church is a lampstand, and only Christ Himself can be the lamp upon it. Unlike us who hang our lamps from the ceiling, the Jewish people in ancient times set their lamps on lampstands. The Bible likens the church to a lampstand. This signifies that Christ has put Himself into the church and that God, who dwells in Christ and who passes through Christ, shines forth through the church. Furthermore, a lamp is mainly used during the dark night. The cities and localities on the earth are full of darkness, but God as the light is in Christ, Christ as the lamp is in the church, and the church has become the lampstand shining forth the light, which is God in Christ. This is what God desires to do in this age in locality after locality.

We must be clear about the two kinds of lampstands at the beginning and at the end of Revelation. At the beginning, the lampstands are small, but at the end the lampstand is large, and at the beginning the lampstands are numerous, whereas at the end the lampstand is unique. However, in principle, all of the lampstands have Christ as the lamp and God as the light within the lamp. Furthermore, the existence and formation of all the lampstands, whether small or great, are due to the fact that they have passed through trials. The great lampstand, the New Jerusalem, is constructed with precious stones, which are produced through heat and pressure, and the seven small lampstands were produced from gold that had been burned and beaten.

What we have mentioned above are the similarities of the lampstands. All the lampstands have Christ as the lamp and God as the light within and are produced out of the divine life and divine nature through burning heat, heavy pressure, beating, and testing. However, there are also differences. First, they are different in measure. The seven lampstands are small, but the unique lampstand is large. Second, they are different in time. The one large lampstand will exist in eternity future, but the seven small ones exist in the present age. The third difference is in location. The great lampstand will be in the new heaven and new earth, but the seven small ones are located in different cities and localities. The fourth difference is in their constituents. The great lampstand comprises not only the saints in the New Testament church, represented by the twelve apostles, but also the Old Testament saved ones, represented by the twelve tribes of Israel. It is built with all the saved ones throughout the generations in both the Old Testament and the New Testament who have passed through trials and have been built into this great lampstand. The seven small lampstands refer only to the saved ones in various cities and localities in the New Testament age. Therefore, the two kinds of lampstands are the same in nature and principle but different in measure, time, location, and constituents. I believe that we all have been deeply impressed with these two pictures of the small lampstands and the great lampstand.

NEEDING TO BE BUILT IN THE LOCAL CHURCHES

Now I would like to raise a question. We have pointed out many times that the great lampstand, the New Jerusalem, is the issue of God's work throughout the ages. After the creation of the heavens and the earth, God began the work of building. God has only two kinds of work in the universe—the first kind is creation, and the second is building. After doing a work of creation, God began to do His work of building, first in the Old Testament age and then in the New Testament age. He will continuously build until the fullness of the times, which is when He will produce a great lampstand, the holy city New Jerusalem, to be His eternal habitation and also Christ's bride and counterpart. This is the ultimate goal of God's work. The small lampstands are merely the result of God's building work in different localities in the present age. Then into which lampstand should we who have received grace and are living in this age be built? Should we be built into the great lampstand, or should we be built into the small lampstands?

Let me give the background behind this question. In the past several decades we have been paying particular attention to the matter of the church among God's children. Because of this, we have frequently encountered questions and arguments from many brothers and sisters outside the recovery. These ones are quite zealous for the Lord. They love the Lord, preach the gospel, help others, teach the Scriptures, and lead people to be spiritual, yet they greatly neglect the matter of the church. We consider every spiritual work in all their different aspects to be good, but they must be for the church. These friends of ours in the Lord argue with us, saying, "When we preach the gospel, is it not for the church? When we lead the believers to be spiritual, is it not also for the church? Those who are saved through our preaching of the gospel will be a part of the New Jerusalem, and those who are saved through your preaching of the gospel will likewise have a part in the New Jerusalem. Therefore, are we not doing the same work?" This kind of argument sounds very reasonable, but it is here that a problem arises. Today many of God's children speak with the same tone, saying, "The reality of the church is in the future, so there is no need to take care of the matter of the church today. To care about the matter of the church is too troublesome. We only need to diligently preach the gospel and lead people to be saved, to be zealous, and to love the Lord. This is good enough, because we will all end up in the New Jerusalem in the future. It does not matter where we meet today. When two or three meet at a home in one accord, zealously loving the Lord, praying, and reading the Scriptures, this is also the building. It is not necessary to build the church in a certain locality. Such outward building in a locality is not important. Since we are all going to be in the New Jerusalem, why do we need to look for trouble by paying attention to the matter of the building of the church today?"

Once someone personally said to me, "Thank the Lord that He has raised up a group in China such as yours. Your preaching of the gospel is very good, and your ministering of the word is also excellent. We have read the books published by your book room, and we even use some of them to preach in our church. There is only one matter that is not so good." I immediately understood what he meant, but I still asked him, "What is it that is not so good?" He said, "It is the matter of the church. If you would simply not talk about the church, everything would be fine. Whenever you bring up the matter of the church, there are problems."

I admit that he was absolutely right. I can give an example as a confirmation. The Christians who do not meet with us will buy the books that we publish as long as the books are on being spiritual. They will not buy any book that has the word *church* in its title. Previously, we had published a book whose original title had been *Being Holy and Without Blemish,* and many copies were sold. Christians everywhere bought that book. Later, we thought that the title of this book did not fit its content very well, so we changed its title to *The Glorious Church.* It was the same book, and the content was unchanged. Only the title had been changed. Strangely, however, very few people bought it. We can see that today God's children like to be spiritual, but they avoid talking about the church.

When I went abroad recently, I came in contact with quite a few Western friends. One day I had an honest conversation with one of them. He said, "Brother Lee, in recent years quite a few Western missionaries have gone to China. Many of them have come back to the West and testified that we have to thank the Lord for raising up your work in China in the East. Your work is truly wonderful, but...." When he said the word *but,* he had a sorrowful expression on his face. I immediately said to him, "Dear friend, I know what you were going to say. You were going to say that our work is wonderful except for our speaking on the matter of the church." In the eyes of those missionaries, our work was like a fragrant ointment. Everything in our work was good, whether it was our gospel preaching, our messages for edification, our spiritual pursuit, or the light that we brought forth in our biblical expositions. The only thing that annoyed them was the matter of the church, which was like a dead fly in the sweet ointment. Whenever I encountered this kind of questioning, I had no way to answer them.

Today many of God's children are not willing to talk about the church, even those who work for the Lord. They think that it is enough to lead people to be saved and to be spiritual and that the matter of the church can wait until the New Jerusalem is manifested. Today Christians think that they can establish churches anywhere. They think that one can set up a church in his home, and another can set up a church in a factory. A university professor can gather a few students to meet together and to form a church. Some Christians may even come together to be a "non-church" church. These are all theories conceived by the human mind and are not according to God's plan. The eternal plan of God is to obtain a group of people in this age and in every locality who have been redeemed and saved by His grace to be built together in His life to become a golden lampstand that Christ may be the lamp upon it to shine forth God as the light within. God wants to build His church today, not in the future. According to man's concept, to have the church is very inconvenient. However, according to God's economy, having the church is very convenient. Man says that avoiding the matter of the church saves us from problems. God says, however, that without the church, problems will abound. Only when there is the church can the problems be solved.

BEING UNABLE TO STAND APART FROM THE CHURCH

If none of us paid attention to the matter of the church, then what would we do after we were saved? How would we meet, pursue the Lord, or preach the gospel? Consider the church in Taipei for example. Often, we feel that the church is weak. However, because we are continually standing on the ground of the church and living in the principle of the church, whenever we preach the gospel, several hundred people are baptized. This kind of gospel preaching is much more effective than gospel campaigns carried out by a single individual. Of course, there are some brothers and sisters who are not satisfied with the condition of the church. They criticize the church, saying that the church meetings are too dead, the ministering of the word is too weak, the responsible ones are short of love, the prayer meetings put the saints to sleep, and the Bible studies and times of fellowship among the saints are meaningless. They also complain that it takes two and a half hours of traveling to go to a meeting and that it simply consumes their energy, strength, and time. Therefore, they would rather spare themselves these troubles and stay in their own homes to read the Bible, pray, and draw near to the Lord. To them, this would be far more enjoyable. Since these calculations seem to fit their economic principles, they decide not to go to the meetings anymore. In the beginning, it may seem very good. During the first week they may read the Scriptures and pray every day, but after two weeks, these practices may begin to decline. Then after two or three months, they may stop reading the Bible. They may also consider the practice of kneeling down to pray to be time-consuming. Hence, they may merely close their eyes and meditate a little, thinking that this is sufficient. This seems rather convenient and economical. However, this was also the economic principle of Judas, who betrayed the Lord Jesus. I am afraid that these kinds of brothers and sisters who are independent and who do not want the church, after making such calculations, will eventually end up in the movie theaters.

You may feel that you are very strong, and you may criticize the church meetings as being poor, weak, depressing, and tasteless. However, try not attending any meetings for two months and see whether or not you can continue to stand. I cannot believe that such a Christian could be so strong and continue to stand alone. I would cry out loudly, "It is impossible!" I absolutely believe that no matter how poor, weak, and depressing the church meetings are, if you would still come to the meetings regularly, the Lord would preserve and sustain you so that you would be able to stand to the end and not grow cold. This is a marvelous thing and an undeniable fact. Conversely, a person who decides to give up the church will fall into spiritual weakness and death. This kind of person may be quick to criticize the church when he is in a peaceful situation—that is, when his business is prosperous, his children are safe, and his family is happy. He may enjoy listening to music at home, and it may seem that all is well with him. I do not mean to curse such ones, but one day the business will go bankrupt, one of the children will die, he will have a car accident, or his wife will be hospitalized. It will seem that all kinds of hardship are coming upon him. At such a time he will remember the church again. Then when the brothers and sisters visit him to pray and have fellowship, he will be greatly touched and exceedingly happy. When he comes back to the meeting, although the condition of the church will be the same as before, his feeling will be quite different. The place that he previously had thought was cold, tasteless, and boring will become the warmest and sweetest place to him.

Have you ever had this kind of experience? Many times you may feel confused and unclear within, and no matter how much you pray and seek the Lord you cannot get clear. However, when you come to the meeting and sit there for half an hour, even though your spirit may be closed and down and you may not care for the saints' prayers and testimonies, mysteriously your inner being will be suddenly opened, and a certain matter that has been unclear to you, though you prayed about it for months, will suddenly become clear after the meeting. It might be a sentence in a brother's prayer that opens up your understanding, or it might be a sentence in a sister's testimony that suddenly enlightens you. Such cases are innumerable.

GOD'S SUPPLY AND BLESSING BEING IN THE CHURCH

Even a person like me who speaks for God is dependent upon the supply of the saints. Even the messages that I give come from the saints. If I were to keep myself in isolation and not meet with the saints or have frequent contact with them, then I believe that after half a year I would have no messages to give. I frequently attend the meetings in the various halls and homes to listen to the prayers and testimonies of the saints in order to collect material for my speaking. I want to thank you all because the messages that I give are supplied by you. We cannot minister the word apart from the church. Outwardly, it may seem that I am giving messages to the church, but actually the church is supplying me with the messages. Even your coming here to listen to the messages is a supply to me. If you all declared a strike and left the meeting, leaving me to look at the empty chairs, I would surely be unable to give a message.

We must see this great matter of the church! According to their human economic principles, Christians consider the church to be too troublesome. They do not want to be bothered by the church today. They think that in the future we will all enter the New Jerusalem anyway. However, the divine economy is not like this. God's intention is that in this age a lampstand for His Son would be built up in every locality, regardless of how many believers are in that locality. As long as there is the building up of the church, the presence, the blessing, and the expression of the abundant grace of God will be there. The supply and the blessing of God are in the church. All of the spiritual supply and blessing is brought in through the church.

The last time I went to America, I met many friends on both the East and the West coasts. When we met, we immediately began talking about the matter of the church. They all lamented and said, "Brother Lee, organized Christianity cannot meet God's need in this age, and the universal church—which transcends time and space, is heavenly and spiritual and will be manifested as the New Jerusalem in the future—also cannot meet the Lord's need today. Furthermore, being spiritual in an independent way, no matter how high the degree of spirituality, cannot meet the Lord's need today." It is amazing that at the end of our conversations, these Western friends all asked me the same question. The question they asked was, "Brother Lee, how can we have a church today that is truly according to God's desire?" They had heard that God had raised up a group of brothers in the East who had recovered this matter to some extent and who had also had quite a bit of experience in this matter. Hence, they were very eager to fellowship with me to receive some help. Now there are many brothers and sisters in the West who have this kind of feeling. They long to be able to have a real and practical church in various localities to meet the Lord's need today.

Please remember that when we are speaking of the practical church, we are not referring to the great lampstand at the end of Revelation. Rather, we are referring to the seven small lampstands at the beginning of Revelation. We should thank and praise the Lord that today in nearly every major city or town on the island of Taiwan, from the east to the west and from the south to the north, there is a church, a small lampstand. The total number of churches is over fifty. This is the practical church manifested in various localities. Therefore, we have to clearly see that the Lord is not waiting for the future to build us into the great lampstand. Instead, the Lord is building us into the small lampstands in the localities that we are in today. God's intention and economy are to have the small lampstands first, and then He will have the great lampstand. First He will have the small golden lampstands in different localities, and then ultimately in the New Jerusalem there will be the great lampstand of precious stones. Therefore, we must not vainly talk about matters in the future. We need to talk about the matter of the practical building at the present time. We need to be led to be built together in the local church where we live.

REJECTING OUR OWN CHOICES
THAT WE MAY BE BUILT

We need to continue learning to be built together in the church in our locality by rejecting our own choices and tastes. I have encountered some brothers and sisters who hope that the church in their locality will go along with them in everything. Otherwise, they will criticize the church or plan to leave. This is not right. We should consider others first and not ask others to consider us. In the church we must repudiate our own feelings. Only then can we have the real building. Since you have consecrated yourselves, I would like to speak a few frank words to you. If you want to be built, do not expect to be delicately treated in the church, like a flower, always expecting that everyone and everything is for you alone. Do not expect that the garden, the flowerpot, and even the soil and water are all for you. If the only purpose of the church was to cultivate you as a beautiful flower, then there would never be any real building.

We are not flowers to be admired and praised. Instead, we are pieces of material—some being wood and others being stone. Therefore, we should commit ourselves without reservation into the hand of God who is the Craftsman, allowing Him to do the work of breaking first. Sometimes He may cut us with an axe, other times he may shave us with a plane, and still other times He may use a saw on us. If God places us in

Keelung, then that is the best place for us. If God puts us in Taipei, where every elder gives us a long face, then that is the best place for us. Perhaps the long faces are the treatment we need. If we truly want to be built, we need to be pressed, even to the point of nearly suffocating, for an extended period of time in the church. While shedding tears, we may pray, "O Lord, I want to be built. Save me from my self and from being natural." In the church we need to learn not to hold on to our own choices. We should not choose the people with whom we want to be, nor should we choose the place where we want to be. Rather, we should be willing to commit ourselves into the hand of the Craftsman, silently allowing Him to work on us, carve us, deal with us, break us, and thereby perfect us and build us together with others. If every brother and sister was like this, how glorious the church would be! Our glorious Lord would be expressed in the church, and the light of God would shine forth in Christ through the church.

ACCEPTING THE AUTHORITY IN THE CHURCH
IN ORDER TO BE BUILT

Now I would like to remind you of another point. If we want to be built, we must accept the authority in the church. It is regrettable that very few among God's children have seen this matter, which is clearly revealed in the Word. The Lord said in Matthew 16 that He would build His church (v. 18). Then in Matthew 18 the Lord referred to the fact that in the local church there is the matter of authority. He said, "Moreover if your brother sins against you, go, reprove him between you and him alone. If he hears you, you have gained your brother. But if he does not hear you, take with you one or two more, that by the mouth of two or three witnesses every word may be established. And if he refuses to hear them, tell it to the church; and if he refuses to hear the church also, let him be to you just like the Gentile and the tax collector" (vv. 15-17). We must see that this is a matter of authority. In this situation there was a brother who had sinned and who refused to repent. Finally, the church spoke to him, and when he still would not listen, the church considered him as a Gentile and tax collector. This is the authority in the church.

Deputy Authority Being in the Church

From reading the Scriptures we can also see that there is deputy authority in the church. For instance, in Jerusalem there were initially three thousand saints, and then five thousand more were saved. In addition, more people were subsequently saved. Thus, there were probably ten or twenty thousand saints in the church in Jerusalem. Suppose that one day a problem like that described in Matthew 18 occurred, and someone wanted to tell it to the church. How would he do it? Would he do it by gathering the ten or twenty thousand saints together, making a public announcement, and then asking the saints to vote by raising their hands? To do this would be too troublesome. I absolutely believe that it was not done this way. Rather, in the church there were some who were deputy authorities, spiritual leaders in the church. Telling the problem to God's representative authorities in the church equals telling it to the church.

We can see a hint of this revelation in Matthew 18, but this hint is not clear enough. (This is always the pattern in the Scriptures; when a truth is first mentioned, only a hint is shown, but the second time it is mentioned, it is a little clearer, and the third time it is even more clear. Then finally it is fully revealed.) Acts 7 mentions that the offerings of material goods in the church were committed to the elders. This is proof that the elders are the deputy authorities in the church. They have the authority to handle and decide the affairs of the church. Then in the Epistles the apostles explicitly said that the elders are a group of people who oversee the church. The administrative power in the church is altogether upon them. Therefore, the elders are without a doubt the deputy authorities that God has established in the church.

The Authority of Order Also Being in the Church

In the church there are not only elders who are God's deputy authorities, but there are also many older brothers and sisters who are authorities over us. This is similar to the relationship among the members of the body. Consider my hand for example. Above the five fingers is the palm, which has authority over the fingers. However, above the palm is the lower arm, and above the lower arm is the upper arm, and above the upper arm is still the head. There is authority all the way down the line. If one day my little finger were to say to my palm, "I am not happy with you," this would be troublesome. If the fingers were to say, "We are good friends with the palm, but we are enemies with the arm," this would also not be acceptable.

In the church there is authority and also order. Due to Satan's rebellion, the order in the universe has been thrown into confusion. Due to man's rebellion and sin, the earth is also full of confusion. In today's families, schools, businesses, and factories, in entire societies and nations, and even over the whole globe, there is quarreling and contention. This is because no one is willing to submit to authority, and as a result, no one keeps the order or maintains the arrangement.

As those who have been saved by God and who are living in the church, we need to be the lampstands of Christ and the vessels of God's glory shining for God on the earth. How could we be like the worldly people, not submitting to authority or keeping the order and always quarreling? Today in the world people talk about being democratic and free, but it must not be so in the church. In the church there should be a peaceful, orderly situation. Whenever the brothers and sisters are together, each one should keep the order and take his proper place, whether he is above or below others or on the right or the left. When such a situation exists, then there will be the church and the expression of Christ, the expression of God.

One time someone told me that a certain worldly organization was unable to successfully hold business meetings. Then some of their leaders came to our service meetings to observe us. They saw that the number of people in our meetings was about the same as the number in theirs but that our meetings were very simple. There was no one shouting and no one maintaining the order. The brothers simply stood up one by one to speak without arguing or contending. The business leaders studied us for a while and then told us, "Now we have learned how to hold a meeting." I asked them, "What have you learned?" They replied, "First, we will sing two songs, then we will keep silent for two minutes, and then we will start our discussion. In this way we will be the same as you." I thought to myself, "Go ahead and sing. Even after singing twenty-eight songs, you still will not be the same as us. On the contrary, I am afraid that the more you sing, the more you will quarrel."

Why is it that in the proper local churches there is peace and order? We have to admit that first it is because Christ, the Head of the church, is reigning among us. Thus, the Holy Spirit can freely operate among us and fully be with us. Second, it is because of the fact that the deputy authorities, the elders, whom God has established in the local churches are able to administer and lead the congregation in the Holy Spirit. Third, it is because all of God's children in the churches keep the order. Each one takes his position and submits to one another. No one is proud or conspicuous, nor is anyone self-depreciating or withdrawn. Each one knows what kind of member he is in the Body of Christ, and each one learns in the grace of God to coordinate with others and to be built together. No one acts disorderly or recklessly.

Some might say, "Is this not too authoritarian? Is this not undemocratic?" In God's house there is never the question of whether this is authoritarian or democratic. In God's house there is only the question of God's authority and order. This is the same as the situation in a family. In a family the father and mother are above the children, and the brothers and sisters are in their order, each one knowing his or her position. There is no need for anyone to fight for his or her place. It is not a matter of the elder brother or sister being authoritarian or of the younger siblings losing their freedom. It is altogether not such a matter.

SUBMISSION TO AUTHORITY
BRINGING IN THE LORD'S PRESENCE

Suppose that the elders in a church decide to study the book of Romans together in the meetings, but a few of the brothers and sisters speak out against it and suggest studying Ephesians instead. On the surface this may seem to be a small matter, but it violates a great principle. It proves that those brothers and sisters have not learned the lesson of submission and have not known authority and order. If all the brothers and sisters were like this, how could there not be contentions in the church? Once there is contention, we lose the presence of the Holy Spirit and fall short of the glory of God. On the contrary, if all the brothers and sisters would learn the lesson of submission and recognize the authority and order in the church, then, whether the elders decide to study Romans or any other book or decide to do something else, they would all receive it joyously from the heart. If there were such a harmonious situation, then it would surely bring in the full presence of the Lord, and the glory of God would fill the church.

Do not think that the authority in the church is a small matter. Let me give another example to illustrate this matter. Suppose that the sisters come to the meeting hall to clean and wipe the chairs. The responsible brother previously told the sisters that the paint on the chairs is not waterproof and that they should use dry cloths, not wet cloths, to wipe the chairs. However, one sister who has never been in the cleaning service but who recently became zealous also comes to clean. Because she did not understand the instructions, she uses wet cloths to clean the chairs. The sister who is in charge of cleaning knows that this sister is like a goldfish bowl that looks beautiful but is very fragile and cannot be touched, because once it is touched, it breaks. Therefore, she very carefully and with a gentle voice asks the sister to use dry cloths to wipe the chair instead. Unfortunately, after being adjusted, the sister speaks up. She says, "I came to the meeting hall to clean the chairs, so why are you criticizing me? Is it not better to wipe the chairs with a wet cloth? Is the church practicing dictatorship? Is this how you oppress the believers?" Consequently, she does not come to clean the next week and later even stops coming to the meetings because she thought that the church was too undemocratic.

Do you love the Lord with your whole heart? Are you willing to serve the Lord? Do you want to see the church built up soon? Then you must accept the breaking, tearing down, and subduing of the cross. Only in this way can you submit to the deputy authorities in all things, keep the order arranged by the Lord, coordinate in harmony with the saints, and be built in one accord unto the Body of Christ in its full stature.

We must also see that we can learn this practical lesson only in the church. It is not easy to learn this lesson in other settings. If we would seriously learn these lessons, then when we preach the gospel, how powerful we would be! When we open and read the Word of God, how much light there would be! We would see how blessed a place the church is, and whoever comes to this place would definitely meet the true and living Lord. These are the lampstands appearing in various localities. The Christ with all His riches is the light upon the lampstand, and the God of glory is the light within. This is altogether a miniature of the New Jerusalem, manifesting a scene of incomparable glory. This is the work that God wants to recover in this age.

We must consecrate ourselves without any reservation to the Lord. We must offer ourselves wholly for the glorious building work of God in the local church where He has placed us, submitting to the deputy authorities, keeping the order, accepting the limitation of the Body, and coordinating with the saints in one accord until the Body of Christ becomes full-grown for the glorious expression of all the fullness of the Godhead. May God bless every one of us that we may be joined and built together. May He also bless all the local churches that they all may become golden lampstands appearing gloriously in different localities. May the eternal purpose of God be accomplished soon.

ABOUT THE AUTHOR

Witness Lee was born in 1905 in northern China and raised in a Christian family. At age 19 he was fully captured for Christ and immediately consecrated himself to preach the gospel for the rest of his life. Early in his service, he met Watchman Nee, a renowned preacher, teacher, and writer. Witness Lee labored together with Watchman Nee under his direction. In 1934 Watchman Nee entrusted Witness Lee with the responsibility for his publication operation, called the Shanghai Gospel Bookroom.

Prior to the Communist takeover in 1949, Witness Lee was sent by Watchman Nee and his other co-workers to Taiwan to insure that the things delivered to them by the Lord would not be lost. Watchman Nee instructed Witness Lee to continue the former's publishing operation abroad as the Taiwan Gospel Bookroom, which has been publicly recognized as the publisher of Watchman Nee's works outside China. Witness Lee's work in Taiwan manifested the Lord's abundant blessing. From a mere 350 believers, newly fled from the mainland, the churches in Taiwan grew to 20,000 in five years.

In 1962 Witness Lee felt led of the Lord to come to the United States, settling in California. During his 35 years of service in the U.S., he ministered in weekly meetings and weekend conferences, delivering several thousand spoken messages. Much of his speaking has since been published as over 400 titles. Many of these have been translated into over fourteen languages. He gave his last public conference in February 1997 at the age of 91.

He leaves behind a prolific presentation of the truth in the Bible. His major work, *Life-study of the Bible,* comprises over 25,000 pages of commentary on every book of the Bible from the perspective of the believers' enjoyment and experience of God's divine life in Christ through the Holy Spirit. Witness Lee was the chief editor of a new translation of the New Testament into Chinese called the Recovery Version and directed the translation of the same into English. The Recovery Version also appears in a number of other languages. He provided an extensive body of footnotes, outlines, and spiritual cross references. A radio broadcast of his messages can be heard on Christian radio stations in the United States. In 1965 Witness Lee founded Living Stream Ministry, a non-profit corporation, located in Anaheim, California, which officially presents his and Watchman Nee's ministry.

Witness Lee's ministry emphasizes the experience of Christ as life and the practical oneness of the believers as the Body of Christ. Stressing the importance of attending to both these matters, he led the churches under his care to grow in Christian life and function. He was unbending in his conviction that God's goal is not narrow sectarianism but the Body of Christ. In time, believers began to meet simply as the church in their localities in response to this conviction. In recent years a number of new churches have been raised up in Russia and in many eastern European countries.

OTHER BOOKS PUBLISHED BY
Living Stream Ministry

Available at
Christian bookstores, or contact Living Stream Ministry
2431 W. La Palma Ave. • Anaheim, CA 92801
1-800-549-5164 • www.livingstream.com